Classic Four-Block Appliqué Quilts

A BACK-TO-BASICS APPROACH

GWEN MARSTON

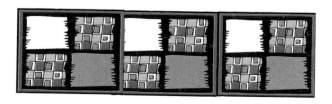

C&T PUBLISHING

Text © 2005 Gwen Marston
Artwork © 2005 C&T Publishing

Publisher
Amy Marson

Editorial Director
Gailen Runge

Acquisitions Editor
Jan Grigsby

Editor
Darra Williamson

Technical Editors
*Rene Steinpress, Joyce Lytle, and
Robyn Gronning*

Copyeditor/Proofreader
Wordfirm

Cover Designer
Kristen Yenche

Design Director/Book Designer
Rose Sheifer

Illustrator
Tim Manibusan

Production Assistant
Kerry Graham

Photography
*Sharon Risedorph, Luke Mulks, and The
Keva Partnership, unless otherwise noted*

Published by C&T Publishing, Inc., P.O.
Box 1456, Lafayette, California, 94549

Front cover: *Tulip Buds in Blue Vase*,
pieced and appliquéd by Gwen Marston.
Hand quilted by Frances Yoder.

Back cover: *Rose and Love Apple*,
Aunt Frank's Tulip, and *Eagle* (detail),
all by Gwen Marston.

Library of Congress Cataloging-in-Publication Data
Marston, Gwen.
  Classic four-block appliqué quilts : a back-to-basics approach /
GwenMarston.
    p. cm.
  Includes bibliographical references and index.
  ISBN 1-57120-275-7 (paper trade)
  1. Appliqué. 2. Patchwork. 3. Quilting. I. Title.

TT779.M287 2005
746.46'041--dc22

                                                    2004018306

Printed in China
10 9 8 7 6 5 4 3 2 1

Dedication

This book is dedicated to the many dear friends
I've made at the Beaver Island Quilt Retreats
throughout the past 22 years.

Acknowledgments

With thanks and gratitude to the quilters who so
graciously shared their quilts with me, and to my
editors at C&T for their enthusiasm and guidance.

Contents

Foreword

When I began making quilts, I began as probably 90 percent of quilters begin: by making traditional quilts using the techniques currently in vogue. My first year of concentrated quiltmaking was under the tutelage of a group of Mennonite women. They were all older women who had quilted all their lives and who had acquired their skills from their mothers and grandmothers. They taught me how to hand quilt, how to use a full-size frame, and how to mark the quilting designs. I am forever in their debt.

Mary Schafer, a well-known Michigan quilter, took over where the Mennonites left off. An experienced quiltmaker, Mary shared her extensive knowledge of quiltmaking and quilt history with me. She also gave me complete access to her quilts, both old and new. This access, perhaps more than anything else, colored my view of what a quilt should be. My careful scrutiny of old quilts began to break down my preconceived ideas about what quilts should look like and how they should be made.

In the early stages of my quiltmaking, I felt I knew what traditional quilts were about. I accepted current ideas such as using commercial patterns, planning symmetrical borders, striving for identical placement of shapes, and so on. The more I studied old quilts, however, the more I began to question my definition of "traditional" as being too narrow. Many of the old quilts that appealed to me most did not fit my original definition.

The antique quilts I studied seemed more original, energetic, spontaneous, and just plain more fun than the contemporary quilts I was seeing. I began to loosen up. My work gradually became freer as I tried to emulate the older quilts. Now, some 25 years later, I'm completely comfortable working with nineteenth-century techniques.

History of Four–Block Quilts

Quilts made from four large blocks were popular from around 1850 to 1890. In my view, quilts from this period exhibit the finest in terms of expertise in workmanship and originality in design. Four-block quilts have a dramatic, bold feeling, quite different from the more formal, delicate designs found in smaller-scale blocks. As a result, they stand out as some of the finest quilts in the American tradition of quiltmaking.

As a group, nineteenth-century four-block appliqué quilts are characterized as being colorful, bold, splashy, original, and spontaneous. Most were florals worked in red and green on a white ground. Popular four-block themes included floral sprays and floral arrangements in vases—at times punctuated with birds and berries—as well as crossed stems, wreath designs, and plumes.

This 36'' x 36'' unquilted block is characteristic—in size, motif, and color scheme—of many nineteenth-century four-block patterns.

Four-block quilts were made in great numbers throughout New England. Pennsylvania also produced more than its share of great four-block quilts, perhaps because the Pennsylvania Dutch adopted this format as a favorite. The Pennsylvania Dutch included German Lutherans and members of reformed religious sects who immigrated to America and became firmly established by the mid-1700s. They were sometimes referred to as the "Gay Dutch" because of their

bold folk-art traditions. With their historical preference for large splashy designs and bright colors, they found the four-block format the perfect design solution for their quiltmaking efforts. These quiltmakers used both solids and small-scale prints, with red and green as primary color choices and pink and chrome yellow as secondary colors. Although most appliqués of the time were worked on white ground, Pennsylvania Dutch quilters sometimes chose colored backgrounds.

This Whig Rose block, detailed from a nineteenth-century Pennsylvania quilt, shows the colored background typical of many quilts made in that region. For a full view of this quilt, see page 103. Photo courtesy of Michigan State University Museum.

These same Germanic people also settled in Ohio, and so it is that Ohio is home to many wonderful four-block appliqué quilts. In fact, women of German descent made 30 percent of the appliqué quilts recorded by the Ohio State Quilt Project.

A particularly interesting phenomenon occurred among the Pennsylvania Dutch quilters. In 1876, America celebrated its 100th birthday, and these women—as many American women did—naturally turned to their quiltmaking to express their patriotism. Four-block eagle quilts, unlike any quilts made elsewhere before or since, became popular. Although no printed patterns have been found, nearly all of these quilts share fundamental similarities. The shape and placement of the eagles, the shield, and the sunburst motif are surprisingly consistent, and a sprinkling of stars appears frequently. Some eagles carry what appear to be cigars but probably represent firecrackers in celebration of Independence Day. Other eagles carry laurel leaves, golden rings, or baskets. I included many of these elements in my *Eagle* quilt (page 92).

During the period when four-block quilts were popular, one-block quilts intended for use as crib quilts began to appear as well. Surrounding a single large block with a pieced or appliquéd border was a natural progression that was very much in keeping with the eighteenth- and nineteenth-century practice of making small versions of full-sized quilts for children. For more on adapting four-block quilts into one-block quilts, see pages 79–85.

My **Eagle** quilt includes many elements in homage to its nineteenth-century roots. For a full view of this quilt, see page 92.

Characteristics of Nineteenth–Century Appliqué Quilts

An examination of nineteenth-century four-block appliqué quilts reveals definite artistic characteristics reiterated in the majority of early appliqué quilts. I list them here in brief, followed by a fuller explanation of each characteristic.

DESIGN

- Quilts are original designs based on formats rather than on commercial patterns.

SHAPES

- Shapes are more likely to be abstract, rather than realistic. They are big, bold, and simple, rather than delicate and refined.

- Shapes are rarely identical.

- Shapes are cut from folded paper templates or directly from folded fabric.

COLOR

- Most quilts are primarily red and green, with the most common accent colors being yellow, pink, or blue.

- Blocks are not necessarily consistent in terms of color. Sometimes the same color is used but in a different tone. Sometimes a replacement color or a print instead of a solid is used.

- Backgrounds are almost always white or unbleached muslin, with the exception of the quilts made by the Pennsylvania Dutch, who often used colored backgrounds.

PLACEMENT OF PATCHES

- Placement and size of individual motifs often vary from block to block.

BORDERS

- Some quilts have four borders, some three, some two, and some just one.

- Some quilts have no borders at all; instead, the appliqué blocks come right to the edge.

- Some quilts have different motifs on each border.

- Most of the corners are asymmetrical. Instead of turning the corners symmetrically, vines "naturally" meander around the quilt.

- Appliqué quilts sometimes have pieced borders.

- Pieced borders don't turn corners symmetrically either; instead, they are often chopped off at the ends. Points often don't match.

Let's take a closer look at these characteristics.

Design

Because many early quilters did not have printed patterns, the appliqués in these nineteenth-century quilts tend to be more diverse. It is hard to find two nineteenth-century appliqué quilts that are identical. Quilters drafted their own patterns, and although these patterns may have been similar, they were not the same. The similarity sprang from the fact that quilters designed their quilts by relying on a few well-known formats, such as crossed stems with flowers, vases full of flowers, wreaths, simple flowers on single or multiple stems, plumes, variations of the Whig Rose motif, and eagles. In addition, there were free-floating shapes to fill the open spaces: flowers, leaves, animals, birds, people, and other shapes. If a quilter decided to make a basket quilt, she designed her own basket shape and filled it with any kind of flower and leaf shapes she wanted. She might add birds or berries—but then again, she might not.

In the days before printed patterns became common, quilt patterns were passed along in families and communities. As families spread out during the westward migration, they took their quilts with them, spreading quilt styles and patterns. State and county fairs were going strong by the 1850s. These fairs provided great family outings. The men came to see the latest in farming techniques and to admire prize-winning livestock. For women, the home arts were the attraction. There were canning displays, cooking competitions, and needlework of all kinds, including quilts. Even though patterns were not available, women paid careful attention to the quilts they saw and tried to replicate them at home.

In the days before printed patterns became common, quilt patterns were passed along in families and communities.

Shapes

For the most part, the motifs found on nineteenth-century quilts are abstract and stylized. These earlier quilts were frequently composed of large, simplified shapes worked in strong color. The results were bold and powerful in their overall design, in contrast to both the fussy Baltimore albums and the soft, refined quilts that came later.

The shapes found on old quilts vary in size and consistency because shapes were cut either from folded paper templates or directly from folded fabric. The notion that the shapes should be identical was obviously not an issue.

Color

The majority of nineteenth-century quilts were worked in red and green on a white ground. Pink, a strong yellow we now refer to as chrome, and blue were common accent colors.

Why were red and green the colors of choice for most appliqué quilts made in the later decades of the nineteenth century? I can think of four possible reasons:

- Artistically, this complementary color combination works.

- Red and green make an obvious choice for flowers and leaves, the subject matter of many of these quilts.

- Red fabrics were colorfast. This fact alone made red a popular choice. By the 1830s, red fabric that held its color was widely available. Green fabrics were a horse of a different color. They were not as likely to be colorfast and often faded to brown or tan. Some of the green fabrics lost almost all of their color, turning to off-white. For evidence of this phenomenon, see the detail of *Plume* at right.

- Color selection was probably a matter of current trends to some degree. That was the fashion, and—then as now—many are inclined to go along with what's "in."

It is obvious that time has taken its toll on the original color of the fabric in this nineteenth-century quilt. For a full view, see page 100.

It isn't uncommon to see early quilts that use color substitution or different tones of the same color. Sometimes the tones are similar, and sometimes they vary dramatically. I assume these inconsistencies resulted when the quilter ran out of a particular fabric and used the next best option to complete the quilt. In other cases, it might not have been a substitution at all, but rather a variation that resulted when a fabric in the quilt faded to another tone over time. Whatever reason for the different tones, I find the effect attractive. I use color substitution in my own work because I think it adds visual interest to the quilt. A slightly different tone of the same color creates a subtle illusion of depth and movement. Even slight differences can hold the viewer's interest longer, which is often a sign of a good quilt.

Placement of Patches

Almost all early quilts demonstrate placement of appliqué patches by eye, with more or sometimes less care. The amount of irregularity varies from quilt to quilt, with some quilts appearing to be quite precise and others obviously very relaxed. However, if you study the quilts that "appear" to be precise, some variation almost always exists.

Borders

The Mennonites who taught me to quilt told me, "A quilt without a border is like a picture without a frame." They believed a quilt should have four borders and that those borders should be symmetrical. As a good student, I accepted their theory—they knew a lot more about quiltmaking than I did!

Later, as I became a dedicated student of old quilts, I began to notice that these quilts did not always follow the rule. I noticed a tremendous variation in how earlier quilters handled the borders on their quilts. Although I did see some quilts with four borders, I also found quilts with three borders, some with two, and some with just one. Quilters might have made three borders because the top of the quilt would go under the pillows and wouldn't show. They might have made just one or two borders, depending on how the bed would be placed against the wall: no sense doing all that work when it wouldn't even show. Although these decisions may have been made for practical reasons, they can work artistically, as you can see by studying many of the fine examples in the Gallery of Quilts (pages 90–107).

A slightly different tone of the same color creates a subtle illusion of depth and movement.

Quite a few antique quilts didn't have any borders at all. They were either pieced or appliquéd right out to the edges. Done. I often honor this tradition in my own quiltmaking; *Tulip With Red-Tipped Leaves* (page 93) is a good example.

Susan McCord is my favorite quilter and, therefore, has influenced my work. She was born in 1829, married, and became an Indiana farm wife. One wintry day in 1909, Susan was milking a cow. The cow kicked her and broke her hip; she never recovered from the run-in.

During her lifetime, Susan designed and made incredibly beautiful quilts from her scrap bag. About a dozen of her quilts are housed at The Henry Ford Museum at Greenfield Village in Dearborn, Michigan. Susan made a pieced Turkey Tracks quilt with just one appliqué border. The border is about 5" wide and is overflowing with little berries and Susan's famous pieced leaves. It is magnificent to behold, and it struck me that making one incredible appliqué border was a great idea. You could put all the energy it would take to make four borders into one border and have something truly outstanding.

WANDERING FOOT OR TURKEY TRACKS, size unavailable, circa 1875, pieced, appliquéd, and hand quilted by Susan Noakes McCord, McCordsville, Indiana. From the Collections of The Henry Ford.

One of my favorite old treatments is a quilt with four borders, each graced by a different appliqué design. Susan McCord used this idea on a nine-block appliqué quilt called the *Harrison Rose*. I decided that if this approach was good enough for Susan, it is good enough for me! My *Whig Rose* quilt (page 83) was inspired by this approach to border design.

HARRISON ROSE, size unavailable, circa 1860, pieced, appliquéd, and hand quilted by Susan Noakes McCord, McCordsville, Indiana. From the Collections of The Henry Ford.

Most early appliqué borders were not symmetrical, nor did they turn the corners symmetrically. In the nineteenth century, vine borders with flowers and leaves were the most common type of appliqué border. I've looked at 389 quilts made between 1825 and 1900 that feature vine borders, and of these, 339 do *not* turn the corners symmetrically. Only 50 of the quilts turn the corners the same way, and almost every one of those shows signs of asymmetry. Even when the corners are fairly symmetrical, the vine itself almost always wavers. Apparently, symmetrical corners were of little concern to the nineteenth-century quiltmaker.

In my study, I observed two main types of vine borders. The first type features a continuous vine. In some examples, the vine travels in an unbroken curving line around the entire border. Most often, however, the vine does not turn all of the corners in the same way.

Rather, the vine meanders along unevenly, fairly lurching around each corner however it can when it gets there. Of the 389 quilts I studied, 267 fell into this category.

The second type of vine border is not continuous; instead, it starts and stops. This type accounted for 72 of the 389 quilts in my study. I believe these borders were the result of a quiltmaker simply doing what was practical. I know from my own experience that it is much easier to appliqué the borders *before* they are added to the body of the quilt. Working on a single border is far less cumbersome than handling the entire quilt with all four borders already attached.

Appliqué quilts of the nineteenth century sometimes featured pieced borders, and pieced quilts sometimes had borders with appliqué. Appliqué and piecing make a good marriage, although this combination was more common in nineteenth-century quilts than in their twentieth-century counterparts.

Like my nineteenth-century counterparts, I often let my appliqué borders stop and start as they may. For a full view of this quilt, see page 79.

Technique

In addition to design sensibilities, construction techniques were considerably different in the nineteenth century. Consider the following:

- Appliqué was done using the needle-turn method. Sometimes edges were basted under first; sometimes they were not.

- White thread was sometimes used for all appliqué, probably because colored thread was not as available as it is now. Most often, the quilting was also done with white thread.

- Binding was usually cut single width on the straight of the goods. It was also common to eliminate binding altogether by turning the top of the quilt to the back with an overcast stitch or whipstitch.

The Nineteenth-Century Attitude

As you can see, it seems that for nineteenth-century quiltmakers, variation in design was considered as legitimate an approach as design demanding exactness. The free-form approach to technique, including folded-fabric shapes and free placement of shapes, also contributed to the spontaneity of these earlier quilts.

This difference in attitude toward quiltmaking is key to the look of these wonderful old quilts. It is hard for me to believe that a seamstress with such obvious and impeccable sewing skills couldn't have turned a corner if she had deemed it important. It's all in the attitude!

In summary, the differences between nineteenth- and twentieth-century quilts may be attributed to two primary factors:

- The **perception of what made a quilt beautiful** differed from century to century.

- The **different techniques used to make the quilts** contributed to differences in their appearance.

Going Back to Basics

Appliqué is a French word meaning "applied." It is nothing more than sewing one piece of fabric onto another—or at least that used to be the case. In earlier times, patches were simply laid on the ground, needle-turned under, stitched, and that was that. If you want the look of an antique quilt, this is the way to get it. You won't get it with freezer paper; in fact, it may come as a surprise to know that appliqué quilts existed well *before* the advent of freezer paper.

One reason nineteenth-century quilts look as they do is the techniques used to make them. I began to use traditional techniques because I wanted to achieve effects similar to those I repeatedly saw in older quilts. By going back to the basics and adopting the traditional techniques, I have learned how to make quilts with characteristics similar to those found in the older quilts.

This back-to-basics approach recalls a time when appliqué was far less complicated than it has become today. Both design and technique were more direct in the nineteenth century. The back-to-basics technique offers a way to work more freely. It is about improvisation. It strips technique down to the bone. By eliminating the unnecessary steps, the work becomes both easier and faster, and you'll unlock the door to creating quilts with nineteenth-century flavor.

Back-to-basics appliqué is easy. It is a simple matter of sewing one piece of cloth onto another—an uncomplicated, direct approach accomplished with the fewest possible steps. It does not require any special tools. You can do it with your basic sewing kit: needles, pins, thread, scissors, and ruler. You simply cut out the patches, baste them on the ground with large stitches to hold them in place, and needle-turn the edges under. In other words, you use the techniques by which appliqué quilts were made in the nineteenth century.

Tools

Within the past fifteen years or so, new tools for quilting have flooded the market. Before that, quilts were made with just a few basic sewing tools: scissors, pins and needles, thread, template material, rulers, and marking pencils. I still make my quilts using these few tools. The only new quilting tools I have added are the rotary cutter, mat, and a collection of Omnigrid rulers.

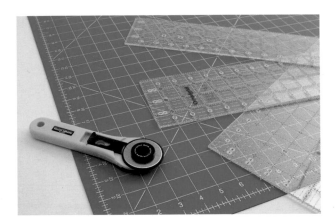

Having the *right* tool for the job is important. Having *quality* tools is also important.

Scissors: There are scissors, and then there are scissors. It is important (and well worth the money spent) to purchase a good pair of sharp scissors for cutting fabric. For appliqué, I have a tiny pair of 4"-long, sharp-pointed scissors. Scissors this size are much easier to handle when making tiny snips. To me, using full-sized shears for delicate, close work is akin to using hedge clippers to cut roses.

Pins and needles: Quilt shops offer an amazing range of choices for pins and needles. I prefer fine silk pins for any piecing or appliqué projects. Silk pins are thin and slip into the fabric easily, without pulling or puckering the cloth.

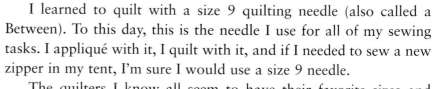

I learned to quilt with a size 9 quilting needle (also called a Between). To this day, this is the needle I use for all of my sewing tasks. I appliqué with it, I quilt with it, and if I needed to sew a new zipper in my tent, I'm sure I would use a size 9 needle.

The quilters I know all seem to have their favorite sizes and brands of needles. You may want to experiment with different needles to see which one works best for you. Keep in mind that the larger the number, the smaller the needle. In other words, a size 10 needle is smaller than a size 9 needle.

One quality I do insist upon is that the eye of the needle must be large enough for me to thread. You'll discover that from brand to brand, there is a surprising difference in the size of the eye of the needle.

Thread: I use 100% cotton thread for hand appliqué. It gives me a sense of comfort to remember that cotton has been used successfully in quilts for hundreds of years. It is also easier to thread a needle with cotton thread than with a blend. Cotton is less likely to fray at the ends, and it won't tangle or knot as easily as cotton-wrapped polyester thread does.

There are several brands of thread available to quilters almost anywhere. Most quilt shops carry either Mettler, Gütermann, or DMC. Mettler makes several kinds of thread, including quilting thread, embroidery thread, and silk-finish embroidery thread. The embroidery thread is my favorite for appliqué, with silk finish being my second choice.

Glazed thread for hand quilting

Thread for appliqué

You may also buy thread specifically made for hand quilting. I like the kind that has a glazed finish, because it makes threading the needle easier, keeps the thread from knotting, and gives the thread strength. You can usually find a good assortment of hand-quilting threads at your local quilt shop.

Templates: When doing *precision* work, you should use accurate templates made from a material that will hold its shape and size. When you make quilts in the nineteenth-century style, however, precision of shape is not a factor; in fact, precise templates actually defeat the purpose. If you are trying to emulate nineteenth-century appliqué, a certain inconsistency of shape is one of the primary characteristics.

If you study antique quilts, it will quickly become clear that the makers did not have accurate templates. Many appliqués were cut with crudely made cardboard templates, paper templates, or no templates at all. All of my quilts in this book were made either with paper templates or without any templates at all.

The "standard" way to cut appliqué patches is to trace around an accurately drawn, finished-size template on the right side of the fabric and then cut 3/16" beyond the pencil line to add the seam allowance. The raw edges are turned under, using the pencil line as a guide. Although I used this method when I first learned to appliqué, I later realized that I didn't need the pencil line to guide me as I turned the edges under; so I eliminated that step. I discovered that because it is almost impossible to turn under more than 3/16" or 1/4", I really didn't need to concern myself with accidentally turning under too much or not enough.

In keeping with the back-to-basics approach, you may also add the seam allowance to the templates. When I make an appliqué quilt that contains repeated shapes, I use this time-saving method to cut four appliqué patches at a time. *Aunt Frank's Tulip* (page 65) contains sixteen large tulips. I folded the fabric in fourths, cut around the paper template four times, and had all sixteen tulips.

> *If you study antique quilts, it will quickly become clear that... many appliqués were cut with crudely made cardboard templates, paper templates, or no templates at all.*

Design

"All art is but imitation of nature."

Lucius Annaeus Seneca
(4 B.C.–A.D. 65)

Artists do not work in a vacuum. They don't sit in a chair with their eyes closed, waiting for divine inspiration. It simply doesn't work that way. Instead, they keep their eyes open to the world around them.

Design ideas are everywhere you look. To a quilter, some places will seem more pregnant with ideas than others. For instance, I rarely look for ideas under the hood of my 1967 Ford pickup. In fact, I rarely look under there at all. Here are some of the places I do look for design ideas.

I look at old quilts. Eighty percent of what I know about quilt-making I have learned from studying old quilts. Antique quilts reveal an amazing amount of information. Not only do they inspire an endless supply of great design ideas, but they also provide solid clues about the techniques used in their making. The result is a gold mine of information that is yours for the taking, if you are willing to expend the effort to pan for the gold.

Sometimes I simply look for specific shapes, such as flowers, leaves, vases, and birds. Sometimes I look for color ideas. Sometimes I study the format of the block or the way the quilt is set together.

I have a growing hunch that nineteenth-century quilt design was very often an outgrowth of the quiltmaker doing what was practical or pursuing the easiest way to complete a particular task. For example, because borders are much easier to appliqué *before* they are added to the body of the quilt, the quilter would complete the individual borders and then add them to the body of the quilt. This seems like a logical explanation for appliqué motifs that run off the ends of the borders instead of continuing unbroken around the entire quilt.

I like making design decisions for practical reasons. Doing what makes the most sense seems wise, whether I am figuring out an issue in my life or making a quilt. I also think working this way may lead to innovative quilts. Instead of blindly following instructions set down by another, my mind is actively engaged in exploring the myriad possibilities. Figuring things out for myself is a lot more interesting and a lot more fun. It is also rewarding in that I get a sense of accomplishment when I successfully arrive at my own solutions. When I paint myself into the corner, I find the most practical way to get myself out.

This brings up my next subject: **designing from mistakes**. When you venture out into unknown and untested territory, that which you hope for doesn't always materialize. As any explorer knows, you must stop, take a reading, size up the situation, and set a new course. It stands to reason that this must have happened with nineteenth-century quiltmakers, which I believe accounts for some of the surprising and unorthodox elements seen in old quilts. I think that when these quilters made a mistake, they didn't just throw in the towel. They forged ahead and finished the quilt the best way they could. Sometimes their "mistakes" yielded unexpected and visually exciting results that rarely diminished the outcome.

Designing original quilts is rewarding and much easier than people think. We have been hoodwinked into believing that there are designers and artists, and then there is "us." Surprise! Designers and artists doodle and borrow ideas from other work just like we do. Consider as well that the majority of the grand antique quilts we admire were designed by *untrained* artists.

My design techniques are based on nineteenth-century methods, are easy as pie, and are completely foolproof. They work for beginning as well as advanced quilters. I know this because I have taught these techniques for many years, and my students have been enormously successful.

Here is an overview of some of the ways I work when designing a new quilt:

1. Sometimes I make a small rough sketch of a basic idea.

2. Sometimes I begin by cutting paper the size of the block, sketching the design on the paper, and refining the drawing. I cut out the paper shapes, pin them on the fabric as I would a commercial dress pattern, and cut out the fabric pieces. If I need multiples of the same shape, I layer the fabric and cut four layers at a time.

What could have been a disaster became a design asset for **Tulip Four Block**. As she worked on one of the blocks for this quilt, quiltmaker Cathy Jones inadvertently cut into the background fabric. Rather than discarding the block, Cathy appliquéd two red birds instead: one to cover the mistake, and the other to keep the first bird company. For a full view of this quilt, see page 96.

Step 1

Step 2

3. Sometimes I draw shapes directly onto the fabric. I mark on the wrong side of the fabric so I can change any lines I wish.

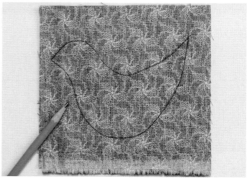

Step 3

4. Sometimes I cut shapes directly from folded fabric or paper without marking at all.

5. Sometimes I design directly with the fabric itself, working out the design as I go. I cut the primary (largest) shapes first, place any stems, and fill in open areas with leaves and smaller floral shapes. I feel free to change the design anywhere along the way.

Step 4

Step 5

Another way to design is not to design at all! Why should you do all the work? Instead of you designing the quilt, let the quilt design itself. This "method" is about trusting the very process of quiltmaking. It is a way of working without planning the entire quilt in advance. Instead, you start with just the seed of an idea and see what happens. Once you get part of the quilt designed, your decisions about what should come next are easier to make, and you can make wiser choices.

Fabric and Color

How to Choose Fabric

Through the years, the majority of quilts have been made with 100% cotton fabrics. Although blends have been used in quilts since the inception of those fabrics, most quiltmakers still prefer cotton for its look and feel. For appliqué projects, 100% cotton fabrics are definitely—hands down—the wisest choice. They are easier to work with than polyester blends, holding a crisp, firm crease for turned edges. In contrast, polyester—by its nature—tends to resist creasing and folding, making it a poor choice for appliqué.

Buy good-quality fabrics for your quilting projects. If you are putting all the necessary effort into making a quilt, you certainly want fabric that will stand the test of time. You can tell good fabric by sight and by touch. The weave will be close and even, with a smooth feel. Some cotton fabrics are heavier and have a coarser weave. These fabrics tend to fray at the edges and are harder to fold and tuck for flat, sharp points. If you are a beginning quilter, I suggest making a trip to your local quilt shop, as they are almost always staffed with experienced quilters who are more than happy to help you.

How to Select Colors and Prints

A number of years ago, my friend Judy Dales and I were teaching together in West Virginia. She had her car, so we made a beeline for the local fabric store. We made our selections and met at the checkout counter. Judy couldn't believe her eyes as the clerk rang up my 10 yards of solid red fabric.

"What in the world are you going to do with *that?*" she asked in amazement. My choice seemed incredible to her. Looking at her stash, I told her the feeling was mutual. She and I make very different kinds of quilts. Our fabric choices are therefore very different.

Because I am rooted in tradition, I look to old quilts as a guide in making my fabric choices. I study the fabrics in these quilts for both color and print. When I am working in the nineteenth-century style, I look at quilts from that period. Often I play it close to home and follow a red and green color scheme. When I am working in the folk-art style, I look at antique folk-art quilts—the colors they include and how they are combined. Today, we are fortunate to have an amazing array of fabrics from which to choose, including repro-

TIP How about using fabrics that you like in your quilt? If you select fabrics that really appeal to you, chances are you will like your finished quilt.

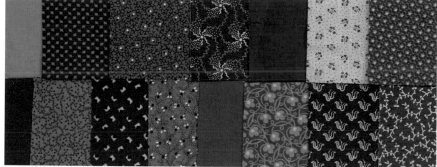

You'll find a wide selection of reproduction fabrics at your local quilt shop.

duction prints from the nineteenth century up through the 1930s.

There is an advantage to having a personal collection of fabrics. For me, it is easier to choose fabrics for a quilt in the privacy of my own home than it is in the quilt shop. Quilt shops have so many fabulous fabrics that I get confused. There is so much to choose from! When I visit a quilt shop, I usually buy fabrics that I like without having a specific quilt project in mind.

I don't have a system for selecting colors and prints for my quilts; rather, I rely heavily on my intuition. When I am ready to make a quilt, I go to my fabric collection and pull out fabrics that I think might work. I place them on the floor next to each other, study them, and try to refine my selections. Often, I choose enough fabrics to get started and then add others as the quilt progresses.

I frequently use two tones of the same color in my quilts. For example, I might choose two reds that are just different enough in tone to add depth and interest to the quilt.

How to Prepare Fabric for Quiltmaking

No one I know particularly enjoys washing and ironing new fabric. In fact, many quilters do not think it is necessary to prewash fabrics at all. However, I think it is best to wash fabrics before putting them into a quilt, especially when using strong colors. I want to make sure the fabric is colorfast. I have heard too many horror stories about the dye in fabric running, and occasionally I have had this problem myself. I'd rather be safe than sorry. Washing fabric also removes the sizing, softening the fabric and making it easier to hand quilt.

It is a good habit to wash and iron fabrics as you bring them into the house. I know quilters who automatically throw all their new fabric in the washing machine as soon as they come home. That way, they know for certain that all of their fabric is ready for use, and they won't need to wonder what has been washed and what has not. Wash your fabric in warm water using a mild detergent. Dry it in the dryer or over the line.

Two different red fabrics add depth and richness to the sawtooth border of **Tulip Buds in Blue Vase.** For a full view of this quilt, see page 71.

Once you've washed, ironed, and folded your fabric, store it away from the light so it doesn't fade along the fold lines.

Cutting the Shapes

With a little practice, you will soon be able to cut many of the shapes for your quilts from folded paper. Once you've experimented with paper, it is an easy leap to cutting shapes directly from folded fabric.

When creating shapes with folded-paper patterns or by folding the fabric directly, there is a certain inconsistency caused by cutting through the multiple layers. If you wish, you may create shapes that are more precise by taking special care when folding and cutting.

When cutting shapes for a specific quilt, determine the approximate size you want each shape to be. If you cut the shape directly from fabric, cut the shape ¼" larger than the finished size all the way around to include the seam allowance.

If you are cutting the shape from paper, you have two options. You may add the seam allowance to the paper template or cut the exact, finished-size template and add the ¼" seam allowance when cutting the fabric.

Cutting shape from fabric with ¼" seam allowance included in the paper template

Adding ¼" seam allowance when cutting shape from fabric

Sit down with some scratch paper and paper scissors to work through the following folding exercises. Pretend you are back in second-grade art class. Be sure to read my little pep talk (at right) first to get yourself ready.

Gwenny's Pep Talk

For many of us, it's much easier to have someone show us how to do something than it is to follow written instructions. When I teach quilters how to cut shapes, I stay right with it until everyone feels comfortable. Although a bit more challenging, you **can** learn how to cut shapes by following these written instructions. If it helps, I suggest you get together with a couple of your friends and work at it together. (I also suggest you do it at **their** houses, as this can be messy business!) Practice with paper until you are comfortable, and then try eliminating the paper and cutting shapes directly from fabric. (Remember, you haven't done this before. If your first try doesn't turn out the way you want, just try again.)

Knowing how to cut shapes this way enables you to create your own original designs—and it's the next best thing to playing with paper dolls. So, once you learn how, spread the word. Offer to teach some classes for your guild or your quilt shop.

Cutting Roses

Roses have long been a favorite motif for appliqué quilts. For these exercises, begin with a 6" square of paper. (When you use these methods to cut shapes for your quilt, begin with a square of paper or fabric the size you want the rose to be, remembering to add the seam allowance.) We concentrate here on cutting roses with six, eight, or sixteen petals. It's easy!

Six-Petal Rose

1. Cut a 6" square of paper and fold it in half.

2. Fold the rectangle into quarters. Unfold and mark one dot in the center of the rectangle on the folded edge and another to mark one-quarter of the rectangle along the cut edge.

3. Fold the rectangle at the center dot so the right corner aligns with the dot marking the quarter.

4. Fold the rectangle again so the left corner is even with the folded right side.

5. Turn the folded paper over, and cut an ice-cream-cone shape.

6. Hold the "cone" by its point to see if the sides are even. Trim if necessary to even out the shape. Unfold the rose.

Step 1

Step 2

Step 3

Step 4

Step 5

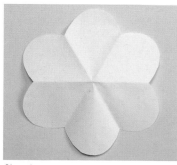
Step 6

Eight-Petal Rose

1. Cut a 6" square of paper and fold it in half.

2. Fold the rectangle in half again to make a square. Notice that two edges are all folds and two edges are all cut edges.

3. Bring the cut edges together to make a triangle as shown. Fold along the diagonal edge.

4. Hold the triangle so all the cut edges are on top. Beginning about ½" down from the folded 90° corner of the triangle, cut an ice-cream-cone shape.

5. Hold the "cone" by its point to see if the sides are even. Trim if necessary to even out the shape. Unfold the rose.

There is a certain inconsistency in shapes created with folded-paper patterns or by folding the fabric directly.

Step 1

Step 2

Cut edges

Step 3

Step 4

Step 5

Sixteen-Petal Rose

Now that you know how to cut a rose with eight petals, cutting a sixteen-petal rose is easy. You need to make only one more fold.

1. Repeat Steps 1–3 for making an eight-petal rose (page 28). Hold the triangle so that all the cut edges are on the top. Bring the folded, 90° corner of the triangle over so that it aligns with the long folded edge of the triangle; fold in place.

2. Ignoring the top point, cut an ice-cream-cone shape from the folded triangle.

3. Hold the "cone" by its point to see if the sides are even. Trim if necessary to even out the shape. Unfold the rose.

Step 1

Step 2

Step 3

Cutting Stars

Stars are folded exactly like roses; only the cutting is different.

Six-Pointed Star

1. Repeat Steps 1–4 for making a six-petal rose (page 27). Bring up the tip so it touches the center of the straight edge of the triangle. Fold in place and mark the cutting lines.

2. Unfold the point and cut directly on the marked cutting lines. Unfold the star.

Step 1

Step 2

Eight-Pointed Star

1. Repeat Step 1 for making a sixteen-petal rose (page 29).

2. Fold point back even with cut edges.

3. Hold the last fold and cut as shown. Unfold the star.

Step 2

Step 3

Sixteen-Pointed Star

1. Repeat Step 1 for making a sixteen-petal rose (page 29).

2. Mark if necessary, and cut as shown. Unfold the star.

 By changing the angle of the cut, you can alter the shape of any star. Try it!

TIP

Cutting Tulips

If you study antique appliqué quilts, you will quickly discover that tulips come in all shapes and sizes. Here are two ways to cut tulips. Try them both to see which you like best.

Sketch a tulip the size and shape you want on a piece of paper. Fold the paper in half down the center of the flower, and cut out the shape.

or

Fold a piece of paper in half. Cut out half a tulip, without drawing it first. Don't be afraid to try this exercise; you are more likely to create surprising shapes. Some you may discard, but others will astonish and delight you.

Cutting Leaves

A good source for leaf shapes is right outside your back door. Take a walk. Look at the leaves. One thing you will notice is that leaves are not all the same size and shape on any given plant or tree. As with cutting tulips (page 31), you might want to try drawing before folding the paper in half and cutting out the shapes. Simple leaf shapes may be cut directly from the fabric without marking.

Take a walk. Look at the leaves. One thing you will notice is that leaves are not all the same size and shape on any given plant or tree.

Cutting Vases

There are many delightfully bizarre vases found on antique quilts. Sketch one the size and shape you want. If you want the vase to be symmetrical, fold the paper in half and cut out the shape. Keep the paper template folded, pin it to a piece of fabric that you have also folded in half, and cut out the fabric vase.

If you prefer, eliminate the paper template and draw directly on the wrong side of the fabric.

Fold the fabric in half, and cut out the shape.

There are many delightfully bizarre vases found on antique quilts.

Placing the Appliqué Patches

The method you use to position appliqués on the ground affects the look of your finished quilt. Some methods result in consistent placement, while others result in varying degrees of inconsistency. Even what appear to be the most controlled of nineteenth-century quilts display some inconsistencies. It is my view that even subtle inconsistency in placement of appliqué patches improves the overall appearance of a quilt. It saves the quilt from the "color by number" look that exactness sometimes fosters.

Free-Placement Method

Our eyes are magnificently designed to do more than we give them credit for. For example, although we are reluctant to use them for this purpose, our eyes can measure distances much more precisely than we think. Also conveniently close at hand—and ideal for measuring short distances—are our fingers. When I am placing appliqués on the ground, I use my thumb and index finger to measure the distance between the shapes, as well as the distance from a patch to the edge of the block. I like the idea of allowing my eyes and fingers to do what they so naturally do.

When I am working in the nineteenth-century style, I want some variation in the placement of the appliqué pieces. Placing the appliqués by eye and with finger measurements gives me the look I am after. Try it: the more you do, the more confident you will become using the natural measuring devices with which we all come equipped.

> It is my view that even subtle inconsistency in placement of appliqué patches improves the overall appearance of a quilt.

"Don't Look Back" Method

The placement of appliqué patches in some antique quilts appears totally random. These quilts exhibit a dramatic discrepancy in the positioning of the pieces. One way to achieve radical placement is to work on sections of the quilt without looking back at what you have done before. In other words, make the blocks one after the other, never referring to the completed blocks. *Tulip With Red-Tipped Leaves* (page 93) was made this way.

Work on the borders the same way—that is, one at a time, without looking back. Study the borders on my *Flower Pot* quilt (page 81). Neither the shape nor the position of the appliqué pieces repeats. All four borders were made independently of each other. One of the benefits to working this way is that you never get bored. There is no repetition, and you are constantly engaged in making design decisions.

"Fold the Ground for Guidelines" Method

This system is so obvious, I'm quite sure it didn't escape discovery by quiltmakers from earlier times. Although it allows for some inconsistency, it is more precise than free placement. You simply fold the ground block in half top to bottom and side to side and then on the diagonal in both directions. You can be more or less meticulous about folding and pressing to achieve more or less exacting results.

The Mary Schafer Method

When I first learned to appliqué, one widely touted method for placing appliqué pieces was to trace the pattern on the ground to ensure exact placement. If you have tried this, you know that it is nigh onto impossible to cover the traced pencil lines completely. Mary Schafer, the great Michigan quilter, has a precise method for placement that is a big improvement over tracing the entire design. She lays the pattern under the ground and puts a tiny, light pencil dot to indicate where the patches begin and end. A dot at the stem and at the end of a leaf is guide enough for Mary to place each leaf in position.

Borders

What can be said about borders? Well, quite a bit actually! The first thing is that you don't *have* to have them. If you opt for the no-border approach, you don't need to read any further in this chapter. If you *do* choose to add a border (or borders) to your quilt, refer to the section on common nineteenth-century border treatments (pages 13–16) to review possible options.

The major difference between nineteenth- and twentieth-century borders is that nineteenth-century borders were usually asymmetrical. If you wish to create the look of an antique quilt, this is one of the characteristics to consider.

I like to postpone design decisions about borders until the interior of the quilt is done. My feeling is that I can make better choices at that point because I have the completed body of the quilt to look at. I lay the quilt on the floor and start toying with different possibilities.

Contrary to contemporary thought, borders do not need to be made from one long length of fabric. They may be pieced from shorter lengths. Piecing borders was okay for the first 200 years of American quiltmaking, so I'm sticking with it! (I feel the same way about not using mitered corners on borders, which were rarely used before 1970.)

Making Borders Fit Your Quilt

I use butt joints for the corners on my quilts. I add the top and bottom borders first, and then sew on the side borders.

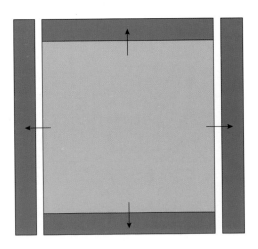

Piecing borders was okay for the first 200 years of American quiltmaking, so I'm sticking with it!

Sometimes I make borders with corner squares, adding the top and bottom borders, joining the corner squares to the side borders, and then sewing the side borders to the quilt.

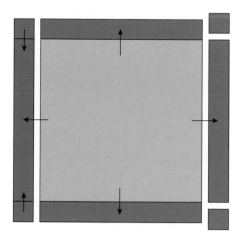

Making borders fit can give a quilter fits. Taking an accurate measurement of the sides of a full-size quilt can be frustrating. Fabric is stretchy, and for a variety of reasons, opposite sides don't always measure the same. Here is the method I use to cope with possible discrepencies.

1. Press the quilt top so it lies as flat as possible. Spread the quilt on the floor or on another flat surface.

2. Measure the quilt down the center, from top to bottom and from side to side. I think this gives the most accurate measurement. I also measure all four sides of the quilt.

"Measure twice and cut once" is an old carpenter's adage. In quiltmaking, I think it is a good idea to measure **four** times and cut once!

My goal is to cut the borders the exact size they should be, based on my measurements. Then I *make* the body of the quilt fit the border. It is worth taking the time to pin the borders thoroughly. If you don't measure and pin the borders carefully, you may end up with a border that ruffles and does not lie flat. I would rather take the extra time and care now, than rip off the border and begin again later.

Here is my method for successful pinning:

Place the border along the edge of the quilt. Match and pin the two ends. Pin the quilt and the border together at the midpoint, and then keep dividing the halves into smaller halves, pinning as you go.

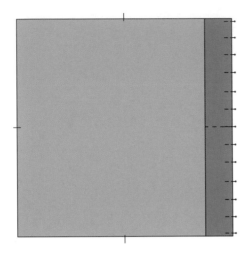

Vine Borders

Read the instructions for Making Bias Vines and Stems on page 44. I like to design the appliqué motifs (leaves and flowers) to fit snugly against, but not underneath, the vine. This makes the appliqué process easier because I can complete the vine and then add the additional shapes one at a time instead of basting them all in place. The pieces don't fray, the needle doesn't catch on the basted pieces, and the whole border unit is far less cumbersome to handle.

If you prefer the stems or leaves to go underneath the vine, baste the vine in position, tuck the ends of the leaves or stems under the vine one at a time, and sew them down. Finish by appliquéing the vine.

TIP

Although I usually cut plain (unappliquéd) borders the exact size I need to fit the quilt, I'll sometimes make an exception if I'm nervous about the measurement on a large quilt. In that case, I mark the exact length I need on the border fabric with a pin or a pencil mark, and then I cut the border about ½" longer. This is like taking out an insurance policy, just in case the border might be a bit short or shift slightly as it is sewn.

When my plan is to complete appliqué borders separately before adding them to the body of the quilt, I cut the borders about 1" longer than needed, complete the appliqué, press the borders, and then cut them to the exact length. I do this because with so much handling, it is possible for the appliqué to pull the border up or for the ends of the border to ravel a bit. These things are not supposed to happen, but in an imperfect world, they sometimes do. If I cut the border a little longer, I can work in confidence, knowing I can trim the ends to an exact fit once the border is complete.

Technique

Simply stated, my method for making appliqué quilts is to add the shapes one at a time, baste them on the ground with large stitches just to hold them in place, and then needle-turn and stitch the edges under. Of course, there is a little more to it than that! I'll lead off with my tips for making your appliqué go smoothly, and then I'll elaborate. How's that?

Gwenny's Appliqué Tips

- Always work in good light.

- Use 100% cotton fabric for both appliqué patches and ground.

- Use 100% cotton thread that matches the appliqué patch.

- Use a needle that is comfortable in your hand.

- Thread the needle with a single strand of thread, 12'' to 15'' long. A longer thread will tangle or wear out.

- Work on a flat surface, such as your leg or a magazine, to stabilize the work. Do not hold the work in midair and try to sew!

- Baste with large stitches to hold the patch in position. Thread basting keeps large pieces from slipping and ensures that you don't work in any fullness in the ground behind the patch. For small patches, I often pin baste.

- Start with a knot under the appliqué patch, instead of on the back of the ground. This is especially important when you are sewing with dark thread on a white ground, as the thread tail may show through the top.

- If you are right-handed, work from right to left. Reverse if you are left-handed. Keep the edge you are stitching parallel to yourself.

- Clip inside curves with a good brand of small, sharp-pointed scissors, but **only** if you need to and not until you get close to the curve.

- Reinforce inside curves with two or three stitches.

- Don't clip outside curves.

- End by tying a knot on the back of the ground. Then slip the needle between the two layers toward the middle of the patch, and snip the thread. This will keep the tail end of the thread from showing through the top.

- Lightly press your work when you are done.

Needle-Turn Appliqué

Needle-turn refers to a method of using the needle to turn under the edges of an appliqué shape as you stitch. Using thread that matches the patch makes the stitches less visible.

1. Hide the knot under the appliqué patch and bring the needle out at the turned-under edge of the patch.

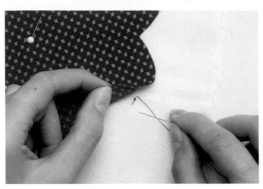

2. Continue to turn the edge of the fabric under by slipping the needle under the appliqué fabric and running it along at an angle. Turn under tight curves about ¼''– ½'' ahead as you sew, and long, straight edges about 1'' ahead.

3. Insert the needle back into the ground fabric exactly beside or slightly behind the exit point and slightly under the lip (or the edge) of the patch. The stitch should be a bit smaller than ⅛''.

4. Bring the needle up again, catching two or three threads on the very edge of the patch. If your needle catches too much of either the ground or the patch, the stitches are more likely to be visible. Make the stitch with one movement, keeping the stitch as tiny as possible.

To Cut Away or Not to Cut Away?

Cutting out the ground behind an appliqué patch is a relatively new technique; I choose not to do it. The reason that most quilters give for using this technique is that there are fewer layers of fabric to quilt. For the modern quilter, there may also be the issue of removing freezer paper.

I think cutting out the ground behind the appliqué patches makes the quilt less stable. If some of the appliqué stitches were to give way, it would be difficult to repair the resulting hole. Another deciding factor for me is how I quilt. I quilt in a full-size stretcher frame. I fear that if the ground were cut away, the tightly stretched top would be pulled irregularly in the frame, and the possibility of threads breaking seems likely.

I don't have trouble quilting through the extra layer of fabric. It is only slightly more difficult to quilt—not enough to make me change my mind. Cutting away the ground is also a time-consuming step that I am happy to eliminate. I have never seen an old quilt that was cut away, and I think there were good reasons why.

Finally, I admit to being skeptical about changing things that have worked wonderfully well for hundreds of years. In the end, this is one of those areas in which we must each weigh the evidence and decide for ourselves.

Saying all that, although I don't cut away the ground, I **do** cut away patches if they are layered—for example, when I am stitching a smaller rose in the center of a larger rose. In this case, I first sew the small rose onto the large rose.

Then I cut away the fabric behind the small rose and appliqué the large, layered rose onto the ground.

5. Pull the stitch through snugly, but not so tight that the appliqué patch puckers and won't lie flat.

Handling Inside Curves

Clip inside curves, if necessary, to make them turn smoothly. I don't clip the curves until I am about 1" to 2" away. If you clip all the inside curves on a patch at once, the edges are more likely to ravel.

1. Using small, sharp scissors, clip about ⅛" into the seam allowance at the curve.

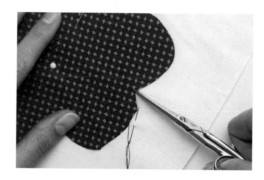

2. Roll the edges of the patch under with the side of your needle, and reinforce the clipped curve with two or three stitches. Take a little bigger bite of the appliqué patch than usual to make sure the inside curve is stable and won't fray.

 TIP The inside curves are the most fragile areas of an appliqué project because there is so little fabric turned under. The few extra stitches you take may be a bit more visible, but you want to make sure that the inside curves are securely fastened and will never ravel.

Achieving Sharp Points

You'll want to make sharp points that lie flat and aren't bulky. Here's how:

1. Stitch toward the point to the exact spot where you wish to turn or change direction. Take an extra stitch at that exact spot to hold it securely.

2. Trim the little protruding point, as well as any excess fabric from the seam allowance, on the side you've just stitched. This ensures that the point will lie flat. To make this delicate work easier, use small, good-quality, sharp-pointed scissors.

3. Turn the fabric point under with your needle by catching and rolling the tip of the fabric with the tip of the needle.

4. Tug the thread slightly, directly away from the point. This pulls any extra fabric out, making the point as sharp as possible.

5. Take a stitch at the tip of the point and slip the needle through the thread loop to form a knot. The knot secures the tip and actually makes it appear sharper. Continue stitching down the opposite side of the appliqué patch.

A student, Miriam Burdick, once told me, "When our needle was too large and thread too long, my home economics teacher used to say, 'You are sewing with a crowbar and a plough line.'"

Step 1

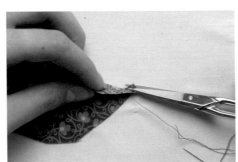

Step 2

Step 3

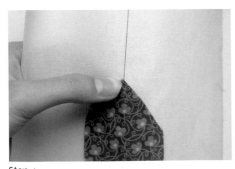

Step 4

Step 5

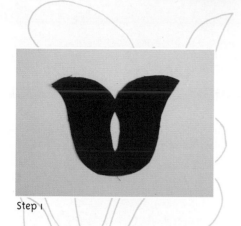

Step 1

Step 2

Step 3

Step 4

Introducing Reverse Appliqué

Even when used sparingly, reverse appliqué adds dramatic dimension to a quilt, and—surprise!—there is no mystery about how to do it. I complete the reverse appliquéd area first, and then appliqué the patch to the ground.

1. Cut the primary shape where you want the secondary color to show through, allowing for an approximate ³⁄₁₆"-wide seam allowance.

2. Cut an oversized piece of the secondary color. I cut the secondary color on the large side because then I know I'll have plenty to work with and don't need to worry about careful placement.

3. Lay the secondary piece on the back of the primary patch, and baste it just enough to hold it in place. Roll the raw edge of the primary piece under with your needle and appliqué it down to the secondary piece. Use thread to match the primary piece.

4. When the reverse appliqué is complete, carefully trim the secondary fabric ¼" from the seam.

Even a little reverse appliqué adds a great touch to an appliqué quilt. In **Horseshoe Plume**, a narrow line of gold accents the tulip appliqués. For a full view of this quilt, see page 79.

Making Bias Vines and Stems

Vines and stems lie flatter and curve more easily when they are cut from the bias of the fabric rather than from the straight of the goods.

A true bias is cut on a 45° angle, but cutting a true bias isn't necessary. Any angle will have give and stretch. Therefore, I never check to see if I have a true 45° angle. Instead, I simply place my ruler at a diagonal that looks about right and use a rotary cutter to cut the required number of strips in the desired width.

1. To make ⅝" finished bias, cut bias strips 1¼" wide with a rotary cutter and ruler.

2. Join the strips with diagonal seams.

I used machine appliqué for the wide, straight stems on **Aunt Frank's Tulip** (detail below). Because they were easy to do, the decision made practical sense. For this quilt, I used a slightly different method than I usually use: I cut the stems finished width plus 1/2'' for seam allowances. I pressed the 1/4'' seam allowances under, positioned the stems on the ground, and pinned them. I set my machine for a small straight stitch and, using thread to match, machine stitched the stems in place by sewing carefully along the very edges.

It was easy (and made sense) to machine appliqué the wide, straight stems on **Aunt Frank's Tulip**. For a full view of this quilt, see page 65.

3. Set the machine stitch at the longest length, such as the basting stitch. Turn both long raw edges of the strip inward (wrong sides together) for the first 3'', overlapping them slightly. You don't need to press.

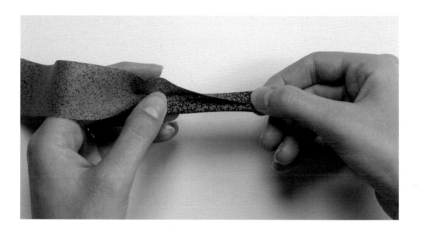

4. Stitch 3'', stop, turn the next 3'', and resume sewing. Continue until the entire strip is basted, and then press. Once the stems are appliquéd, you can easily remove the basting stitches.

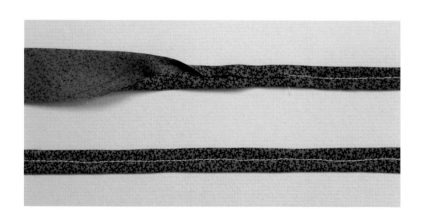

Making Berries

I don't have very many rules, but I *do* have a few. One that I rarely break is "never leave home without your appliqué." When I travel, one of the things I always carry along is a little plastic baggie full of circles to turn into berries for my quilts. These circles are easy to pull out and work on, even in the most confined spaces. I use lots of berries on my quilts, and by making them up in my spare moments, I always have a finished supply ready to use when I need them.

I make berries using the yo-yo method. This method makes it easy to sew the berries to the quilt because the edges are already finished. I also like that the appliquéd berries look padded. I'm often asked if they are stuffed. "No," I reply, "They are just full of themselves."

1. Baste around the edge of the cut circle as shown.

2. Place your little finger in the center of the circle and pull the thread around it as shown. Secure it with a knot.

3. Work the gathered fabric into a circle, using the tip of your needle to shape the edges into a smooth curve. (Sometimes I press the berries, and sometimes I don't.)

When I work on my appliqué in airports, both women and men express interest. When I make berries using my "pull it up around my little finger and tie a knot" method, however, I notice that no one makes eye contact. They obviously think I'm out on a weekend pass, and would rather not know if I plan to make one for all ten fingers.

TIP I often use a large spool of thread as a template to cut the berries for my quilts. I layer the fabric in fourths so I can cut four berries at a time.

Projects and Patterns

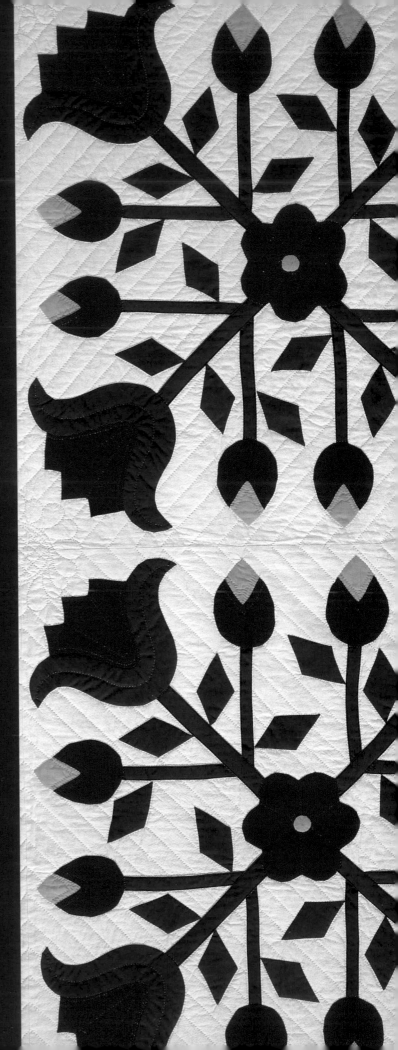

You have several options for using the patterns on the following pages.

- You can follow the project instructions for a specific quilt in typical fashion, using the templates to cut out the shapes and to duplicate the quilt shown in the photograph.

- You can use my back-to-basics methods (pages 17–47) to make a quilt that looks similar to, but not exactly like mine by using the patterns only as a guide for shape and size. For example, if you are making a quilt with a rose shape (such as Rose and Love Apple, on page 50), use the pattern as a guide for cutting the rose from folded fabric.

- You can study the quilts in this book for shapes or ideas you like, and then use them in an entirely new way.

Whichever way you choose to work, remember that your shapes don't need to be exactly like the patterns in this book. Who's to know? Who's to care?

Rose and Love Apple

● Finished size: 57¼" × 57¼"
● Finished block size: 25¼" square
● Finished pieced border: 3⅜" wide

Pieced, appliquéd, and hand quilted by Gwen Marston, Beaver Island, Michigan, 1997.

The Pennsylvania Dutch were known for their strong use of color and for the use of colored backgrounds in their quilts. I've borrowed this idea from time to time, as this quilt illustrates. I outline quilted around the appliqué shapes and filled in the ground with cross-hatching.

Materials

Yardages are based on fabric that measures 40" wide after laundering.

- 3½ yards yellow fabric for block grounds and pieced border
- ½ yard green fabric 1 for stems
- ⅞ yard green fabric 2 for leaves
- 2½ yards red fabric for rose and love apple appliqués, pieced border, and binding
- Scraps of dark fabric for rose center appliqués
- 3⅝ yards fabric for backing
- 62" x 62" piece of batting

Cutting

Cut strips across the fabric width (selvage to selvage).

From the yellow fabric:

- Cut 4 squares 25¾" x 25¾" for ground.
- Cut 32 squares 4¼" x 4¼". Cut each square diagonally in one direction to make 64 half-square triangles for pieced border.

From green fabric 1:

- Cut 1¼"-wide strips from the bias of the fabric. You need 128" of bias for stems.

From the red fabric:

- Cut 32 squares 4¼" x 4¼". Cut each square diagonally in one direction to make 64 half-square triangles for pieced border.
- Cut 7 strips 1¼" x width of fabric for binding.

Appliquéing the Blocks

Block diagram

1. Refer to Making Bias Vines and Stems (page 44), and use the 1¼"-wide green fabric 1 strips to make a single strip ⅝" x 128".

2. Use the method you prefer (either as described in Back to Basics: Cutting the Shapes on page 26, or using the patterns for pieces A–E on pages 53–54) to cut the following appliqué shapes:
   From green fabric 2: 16 each of C and C reverse
   From red fabric: 4 A; 16 each of D and E
   From dark fabric: 4 B

 If you fold the fabric, position template D on the fold. This way you'll cut out both piece D and piece E.

3. Refer to Back to Basics: Placing the Appliqué Patches (page 34), Back to Basics: Technique (page 39), the quilt photo on page 50, and the block diagram above to place and appliqué 4 stems to each 25¾" yellow square.

4. Refer to Needle-Turn Appliqué on page 40. Place and appliqué 1 each of A and B, 8 each of C and C reverse, and 4 each of D and E to each block.

 I prefer to sew the flower centers (B) on the roses (A) before I appliqué the roses to the blocks. With less fabric to handle, it's easier!

Quilt Assembly

1. Refer to the quilt photo on page 50. Arrange the blocks in 2 rows of 2 blocks each as shown. Sew the blocks into rows. Press the seams in opposite directions from row to row. Sew the rows together. Press.

2. Sew the yellow and red triangles together in pairs. Press. Make 64.

Make 64.

3. Sew 15 units from Step 2 to make a border. Press. Make 4.

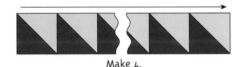

Make 4.

4. Sew a border from Step 3 to the top and bottom of the quilt. Press the seams toward the borders.

5. Sew a unit from Step 2 to each end of a remaining pieced border strip. Press. Make 2.

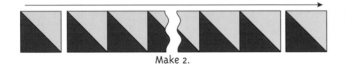

Make 2.

6. Sew a border from Step 5 to the sides of the quilt top. Press the seams toward the borders.

TIP

Designing pieced borders to fit exactly is the easy part. What often happens, however, is that the slightest discrepancy in a few seam allowances may cause the perfectly engineered border to finish slightly too long or too short. The age-old method for handling this situation is to take up (or let out) a few seams, ever so slightly.

Finishing

Refer to Helpful Information for Finishing Your Quilt (pages 86–89) to layer, baste, quilt, and finish the edges of your quilt. Use the 1¼"-wide red fabric strips for binding.

Patterns are finished size. No seam allowances included.

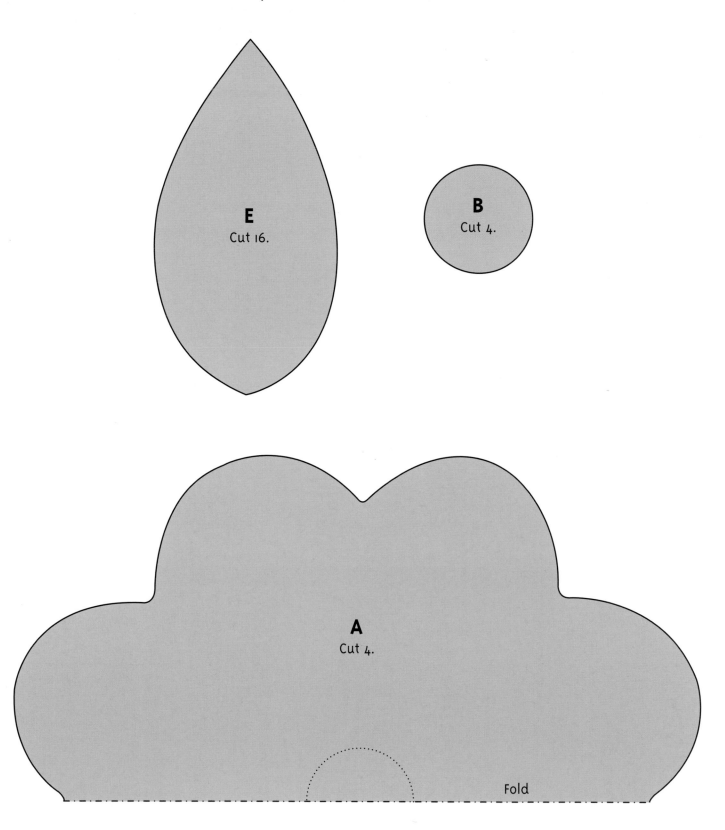

E
Cut 16.

B
Cut 4.

A
Cut 4.

Fold

Patterns are finished size. No seam allowances included.

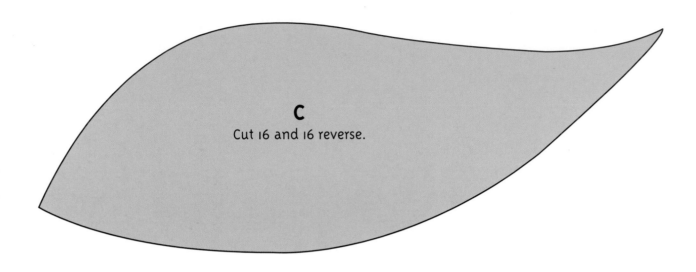

C
Cut 16 and 16 reverse.

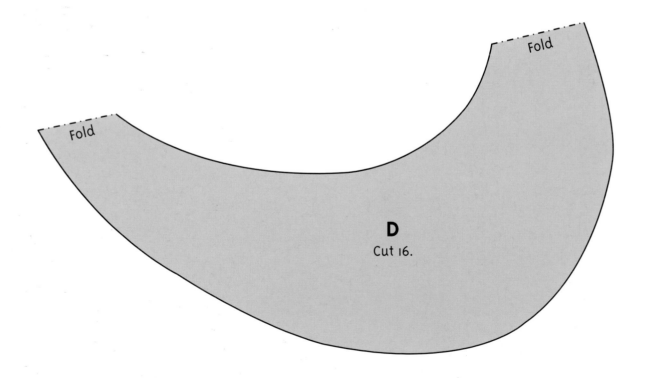

Fold

Fold

D
Cut 16.

Rose and Pomegranate

● Finished size: 61″ x 61″
● Finished block size: 21″ square
● Finished pieced border: 2″ wide
● Finished outside border: 7½″ wide

Pieced, appliquéd, and hand quilted by Gwen Marston, Beaver Island, Michigan, 1997.

This quilt includes both solids and prints in the usual nineteenth-century color scheme of red and green, with gold accents. The block grounds are cut from a small-scale pink print. Quilting is very straightforward: the appliqué shapes are outlined, and diagonal lines fill the background.

Materials

Yardages are based on fabric that measures 40" wide after laundering.

- 2½ yards pink fabric 1 for block grounds
- 1⅜ yards dark green fabric for stems and pomegranate appliqués
- ⅞ yard red fabric for large and small rose appliqués, berries, and pieced border
- 1¼ yards chrome yellow fabric for large and small rose appliqués, pieced border, and binding
- 1½ yards pink fabric 2 for outside border
- 3¾ yards fabric for backing
- 65" x 65" piece of batting

Cutting

Cut strips across the fabric width (selvage to selvage).

From pink fabric 1:

- Cut 4 squares 21½" x 21½" for block ground.

From the dark green fabric:

- Cut 1¼"-wide strips from the bias of the fabric. You need 160" of bias for stems.

From the red fabric:

- Cut 44 squares 2⅞" x 2⅞". Cut each square diagonally in one direction to make 88 half-square triangles for pieced border.

From the chrome yellow fabric:

- Cut 44 squares 2⅞" x 2⅞". Cut each square diagonally in one direction to make 88 half-square triangles for pieced border.
- Cut 7 strips 1¼" x width of fabric for binding.

From pink fabric 2:

- Cut 7 strips 8" x width of fabric for outside border.

Appliquéing the Blocks

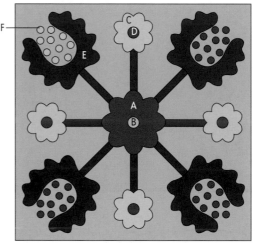

Block diagram

1. Refer to Making Bias Vines and Stems (page 44), and use the 1¼"-wide dark green strips to make a single strip ⅝" x 160".

2. Use the method you prefer (either as described in Back to Basics: Cutting the Shapes on page 26, or using the patterns for pieces A–F on page 58) to cut the following appliqué shapes:
   From dark green fabric: 16 E
   From red fabric: 4 A, 1 C, 16 D, and 120 F
   From chrome yellow fabric: 4 B, 16 C, and 41 F

3. Refer to Back to Basics: Placing the Appliqué Patches (page 34), Back to Basics: Technique (page 39), the quilt photo on page 55, and the block diagram above to place and appliqué 8 stems to each 21½" pink fabric 1 square.

4. Refer to Needle-Turn Appliqué (page 40). Place and appliqué 1 each of A and B, 4 chrome yellow C, 4 red D, 4 E, 30 red F, and 10 chrome yellow F to each block as shown.

Quilt Assembly

1. Refer to the quilt photo on page 55. Arrange the blocks in 2 rows of 2 blocks each. Sew the blocks into rows. Press the seams in opposite directions from row to row. Sew the rows together. Press.

2. Refer to Needle-Turn Appliqué (page 40) and the quilt photo on page 55 to place and appliqué 1 red C and 1 chrome yellow F to the center of the quilt.

3. Sew the chrome yellow and red triangles together in pairs. Press. Make 88.

Make 88.

4. Sew 21 units from Step 3 to make a border. Press. Make 2.

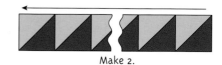

Make 2.

5. Sew a border from Step 4 to the top and bottom of the quilt. Press the seams toward the borders.

6. Sew 23 units from Step 3 to make a border unit. Press. Make 2.

Make 2.

7. Sew a border from Step 6 to the sides of the quilt top. Press the seams toward the borders.

8. Refer to Making Borders Fit Your Quilt (page 36) to sew the 8"-wide pink fabric 2 outside border strips to the quilt, piecing them as necessary. Add the top and bottom borders first, then the sides. Press the seams toward the pink borders.

Finishing

Refer to Helpful Information for Finishing Your Quilt (pages 86–89) to layer, baste, quilt, and finish the edges of your quilt. Use the 1¼" yellow fabric strips for binding.

Patterns are finished size. No seam allowances included.

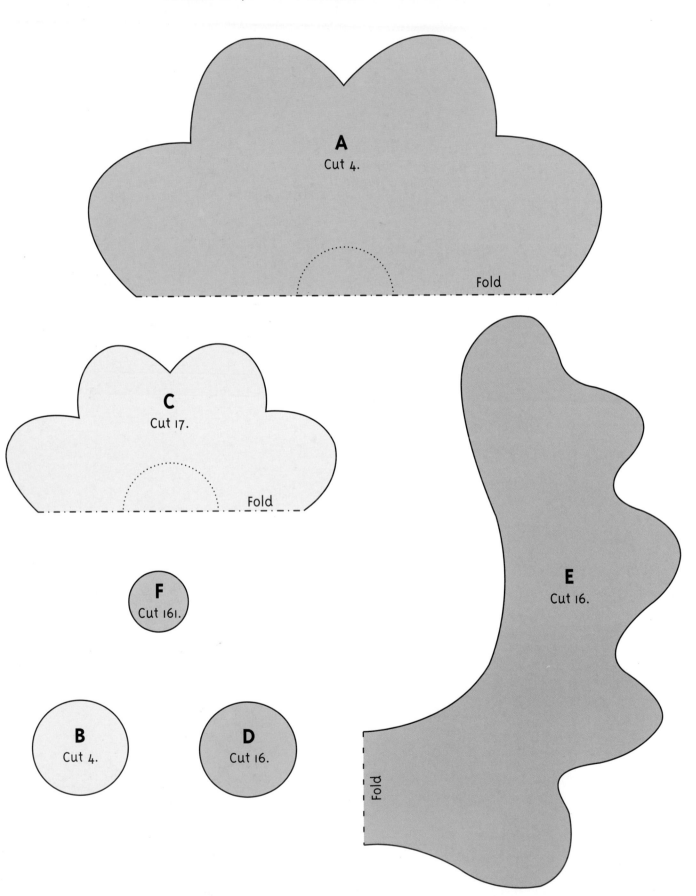

A

Cut 4.

Fold

C

Cut 17.

Fold

F

Cut 161.

E

Cut 16.

B

Cut 4.

D

Cut 16.

Fold

Crossed Tulips

● Finished size: 71'' x 71''
● Finished block size: 18'' square
● Finished sashing: 6'' wide
● Finished pieced border: 5¹/₂'' wide
● Finished outside border: 9'' wide

Pieced and appliquéd by Gwen Marston, Beaver Island, Michigan, 1987. Hand quilted by Gwen Marston and Joe Cunningham.

Over the years, I've seen many nineteenth-century quilts with vibrant reds and greens that have faded to soft rose and tan. I've always thought these quilts were lovely and decided to make a quilt that wouldn't need to age to fade.

Materials

Yardages are based on fabric that measures 40" wide after laundering.

- 5⅛ yards white fabric for block grounds, sashing, pieced border, outside border, and binding

- 1⅛ yards rosy-red fabric for rose, rosebud, and tulip appliqués and pieced border

- 1¾ yards light green fabric for stems, leaf appliqués, and pieced border

- ⅓ yard solid red fabric for rose appliqué and pieced border

- 4⅓ yards fabric for backing

- 75" x 75" piece of batting

Cutting

Cut strips across the fabric width (selvage to selvage).

From the white fabric:

- Cut 4 squares 18½" x 18½" for ground.

- Cut 68 squares 3¾" x 3¾". Cut each square diagonally in one direction to make 136 half-square triangles for pieced border.

- Cut 4 strips 6½" x 18½" for sashing.

- Cut 1 square 6½" x 6½" for center sashing square.

- Cut 8 strips 9½" x width of fabric for outside border.

- Cut 8 strips 1¼" x width of fabric for binding.

From the light green fabric:

- Cut 1¼"-wide strips from the bias of the fabric. You need 140" of bias for stems.

- Cut 3 squares 6⅞" x 6⅞". Cut each square diagonally in both directions to make 12 quarter-square triangles for pieced border.

From the rosy-red fabric:

- Cut 10 squares 6⅞" x 6⅞". Cut each square diagonally in both directions to make 40 quarter-square triangles for pieced border.

From the solid red fabric:

- Cut 4 squares 6⅞" x 6⅞". Cut each square diagonally in both directions to make 16 quarter-square triangles for pieced border.

Appliquéing the Blocks

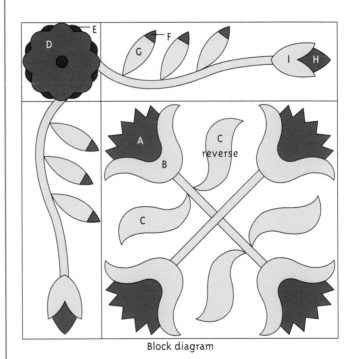

Block diagram

1. Refer to Making Bias Vines and Stems (page 44), and use the 1¼"-wide green fabric strips to make a single strip ⅝" x 140".

2. Use the method you prefer (either as described in Back to Basics: Cutting the Shapes on page 26 or using the patterns for pieces A–I on pages 63–64) to cut the following appliqué shapes:

From rosy-red fabric: 16 A, 1 D, 12 F, and 4 H

From light green fabric: 16 B, 8 each of C and C reverse, 12 G, and 4 I

From solid red fabric: 1 E

3. Refer to Back to Basics: Placing the Appliqué Patches (page 34), Back to Basics: Technique (page 39), the quilt photo on page 59, and the block diagram on page 60 to place and appliqué 4 stems to each 18½" white square.

4. Refer to Needle-Turn Appliqué (page 40). Place and appliqué 4 each of A and B and 4 each of C and C reverse to each block.

Quilt Assembly

1. Refer to the quilt photo on page 59 and the quilt layout on page 62. Arrange the blocks, the four 6½" x 18½" white sashing strips, and the 6½" white center square as shown. Sew the blocks, sashing strips, and the center square into rows. Press the seams toward the sashing strips. Sew the rows together. Press.

2. Refer to the quilt photo and the quilt layout to cut, place, and appliqué 4 green stems to the center of the quilt. Refer to Needle-Turn Appliqué (page 40) to place and appliqué D and E, 12 each of F and G, and 4 each of H and I.

TIP I chose to reverse appliqué the center and inner curves of the scallops of rose E to rose D before appliquéing the unit to the center of this quilt. Refer to Introducing Reverse Appliqué (page 43) if you'd like to try this, too.

3. Sew 2 white triangles to each red and green triangle as shown. Press. Make 68 total.

 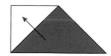

Make 68 total.

4. Sew 15 units from Step 3 to make a border, randomly mixing the red and green units. Press. Make 4.

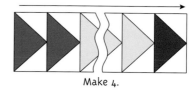

Make 4.

5. Sew a border from Step 4 to the top and bottom of the quilt. Press the seams toward the borders.

6. Sew 2 units from Step 3 to each end of a remaining pieced border strip. Press. Make 2.

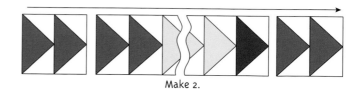

Make 2.

7. Sew a border from Step 6 to the sides of the quilt top. Press the seams toward the borders.

8. Refer to Making Borders Fit Your Quilt (page 36) to sew the 9½"-wide white outside border strips to the quilt, piecing them as necessary. Add the top and bottom borders first, then the sides. Press the seams toward the white borders.

Finishing

Refer to Helpful Information for Finishing Your Quilt (pages 86–89) to layer, baste, quilt, and finish the edges of your quilt. Use the 1¼"-wide white fabric strips for binding.

Quilt layout

Patterns are finished size. No seam allowances included.

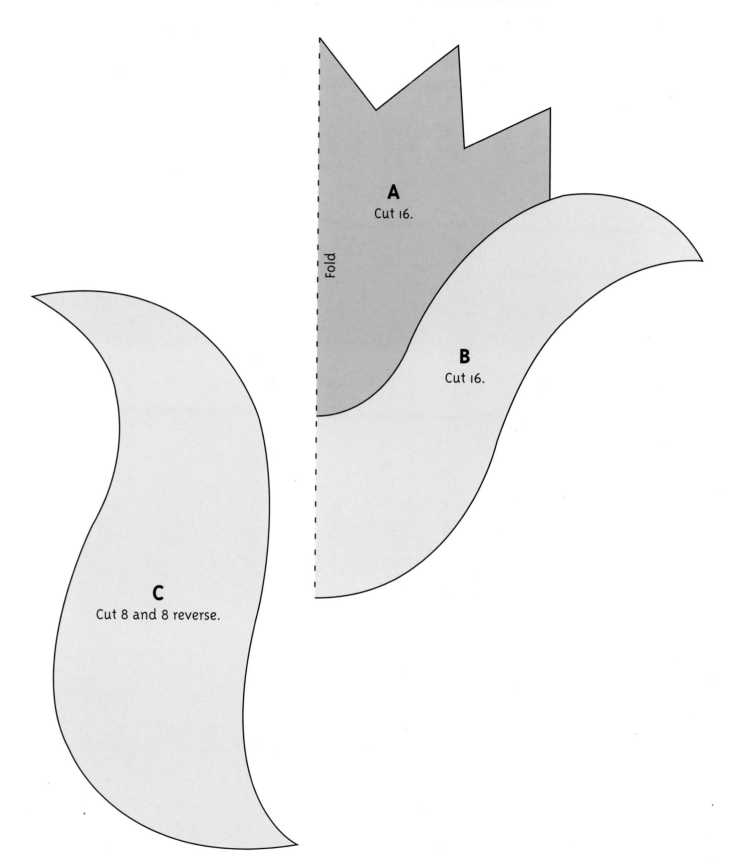

A
Cut 16.

Fold

B
Cut 16.

C
Cut 8 and 8 reverse.

Patterns are finished size. No seam allowances included.

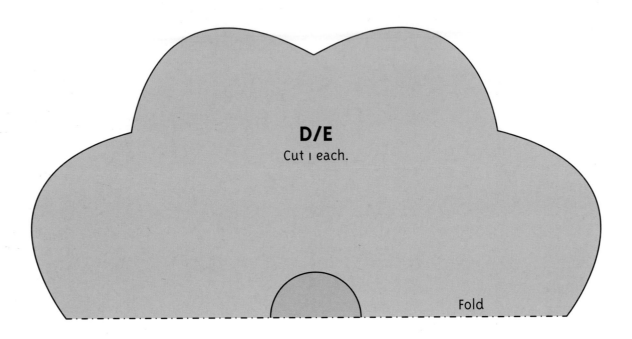

D/E
Cut 1 each.

Fold

F
Cut 12.

G
Cut 12.

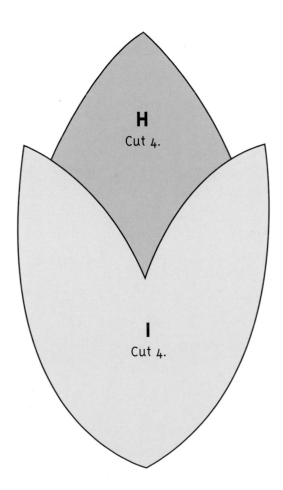

H
Cut 4.

I
Cut 4.

Aunt Frank's Tulip

● Finished size: 62'' x 62''
● Finished block size: 27'' square
● Finished dogtooth border: 4'' wide

Pieced, appliquéd, and hand quilted by Gwen Marston, Beaver Island, Michigan, 1992.

This quilt was named for Frances Tranbarger, a wonderful woman who was my friend and my role model for living an independent life with gusto and good humor. Raised in a large family of newspaper people, "Frank" studied art at Cooper Union in New York City at the same time that Jackson Pollock was a student there.

On one occasion, I stayed with Frank to help her as she recovered from a fall. During that ten-day stay, I had the good fortune of hearing her stories and insightful views about life. I had this quilt cut when I arrived, and by the time I left, the appliqué was complete—a good reminder that quilts with large, simple shapes go together easily, especially when the conversation is so exhilarating!

Materials

Yardages are based on fabric that measures 40" wide after laundering.

- 4⅝ yards white fabric for block grounds, pieced border, and binding
- 2⅛ yards green fabric for stems and leaf appliqués
- 2½ yards red fabric for tulip, bud, and rose appliqués and pieced border
- ⅓ yard chrome yellow fabric for bud and rose center appliqués
- 3⅞ yards fabric for backing
- 66" x 66" piece of batting

Cutting

Cut strips across the fabric width (selvage to selvage).

From the white fabric:

- Cut 4 squares 27½" x 27½" for ground.
- Cut 7 strips 1¼" x width of fabric for binding.

From the green fabric:

- Cut 1¼"-wide strips from the bias of the fabric. You need 256" of the narrower bias for bud stems.
- Cut 1½"-wide strips from the bias of the fabric. You need 144" of the wider bias for tulip stems.

Appliquéing the Blocks

Block diagram

1. Refer to Making Bias Vines and Stems (page 44), and use the 1¼"-wide green fabric strips to make a single strip ⅝" x 140". You will use this bias as stems for the tulip buds.

2. Piece the 1½"-wide green fabric strips to make a single strip 144" long. Press under a ¼" seam allowance on both sides to make a 1"-wide finished strip. You will use this bias as stems for the tulips.

3. Use the method you prefer (either as described in Back to Basics: Cutting the Shapes on page 26, following the instructions in the tip box on page 67 for cutting the diamond-shaped leaves, or using the patterns for pieces A–G on pages 69–70) to cut the following appliqué shapes:

From green fabric: 16 D and 64 G
From red fabric: 4 A, 16 C, and 32 F
From chrome yellow fabric: 4 B and 32 E

 Try the following method for quick-cutting the diamond shapes. These quick-cut leaves already include the necessary turn-under allowance.

1. Layer the green fabric in 4 layers.

2. Use a rotary cutter and ruler to cut a 2″-wide strip.

3. Use the markings on the ruler to cut one end of the strip at a 45° angle. Position the ruler along the angled edge, and cut 16 segments 2″ wide. (Cut and layer additional strips as needed.) Because you are cutting 4 layers at once, you will end up with the required 64 leaves.

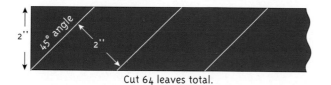

Cut 64 leaves total.

4. Refer to Back to Basics: Placing the Appliqué Patches (page 34), Back to Basics: Technique (page 39), the quilt photo on page 65, and the block diagram on page 66 to place and appliqué 4 wide (1″) stems and 8 narrow (⅝″) stems to each 27½″ white square.

5. Refer to Needle-Turn Appliqué (page 40). Place and appliqué 1 each of A and B, 4 each of C and D, 8 each of E and F, and 16 each of G to each block.

 Tuck the narrow bias stems under the wider stems. I positioned and pinned the stems and then machine stitched the narrow ones first (see Machine Appliqué on page 44) and the wider ones next. I appliquéd the leaves last, positioning them by eye. If you really study the position of the leaves, you will see quite a bit of variation in placement!

Quilt Assembly

1. Refer to the quilt photo on page 65. Arrange the blocks in 2 rows of 2 blocks each. Sew the blocks into rows. Press the seams in opposite directions from row to row. Sew the rows together. Press.

2. Use the pattern on page 70 or refer to the tip box below to cut 116 elongated triangles each from the red and white fabrics. Sew white and red triangles together in pairs. Press. Make 116 total.

Make 116 total.

 If you prefer, use the following method to cut the elongated triangles.

1. Layer the red fabric in 4 layers. If the fabric has a right and wrong side, *be sure* you layer the fabric right side up.

2. Use a rotary cutter and ruler to cut a 5⅜″-wide strip.

3. Cut the strip into 2⅝″ segments. Cut 58 segments. Cut each segment once diagonally to make 116 elongated triangles.

4. Repeat Steps 1–3 with the white fabric to cut 116 white triangles.

2 ⁵/₈″

5 ³/₈″

Cut 58 segments each from red and white fabrics. Cut each segment into 2 elongated triangles (116 each).

3. Sew 27 units from Step 2 to make a border. Press. Make 4.

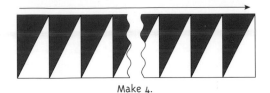

Make 4.

4. Sew a border from Step 3 to the top and bottom of the quilt. Press the seams toward the borders.

5. Sew 2 units from Step 2 to each end of a remaining pieced border strip. Press. Make 2.

Make 2.

6. Sew a border from Step 5 to the sides of the quilt top. Press the seams toward the borders.

Finishing

Refer to Helpful Information for Finishing Your Quilt (pages 86–89) to layer, baste, quilt, and finish the edges of your quilt. Use the 1¼" white fabric strips for binding.

Patterns are finished size. No seam allowances included.

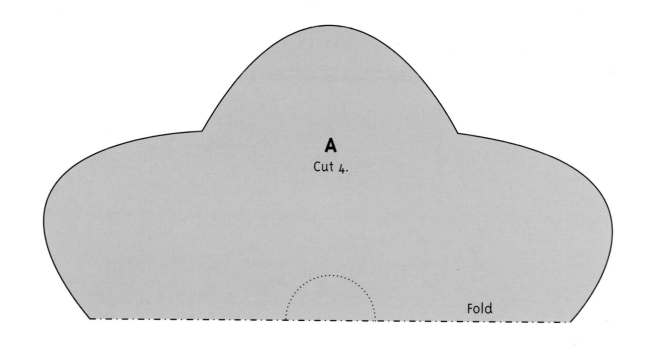

A
Cut 4.

Fold

G
Cut 64.

E
Cut 32.

B
Cut 4.

F
Cut 32.

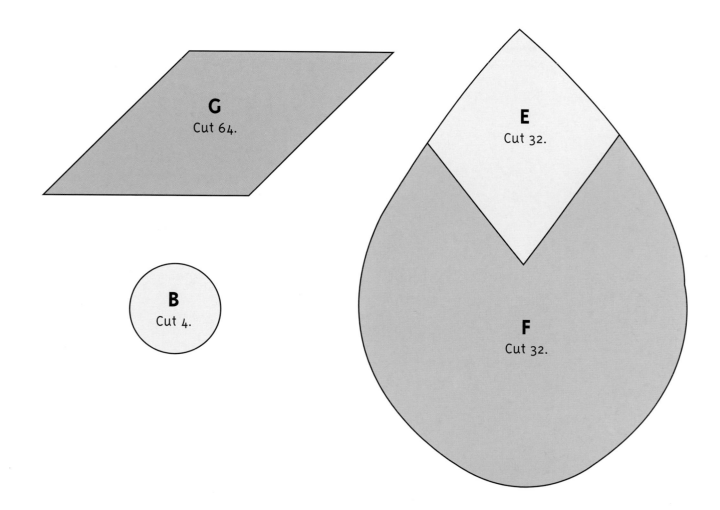

Patterns are finished size. No seam allowances included.

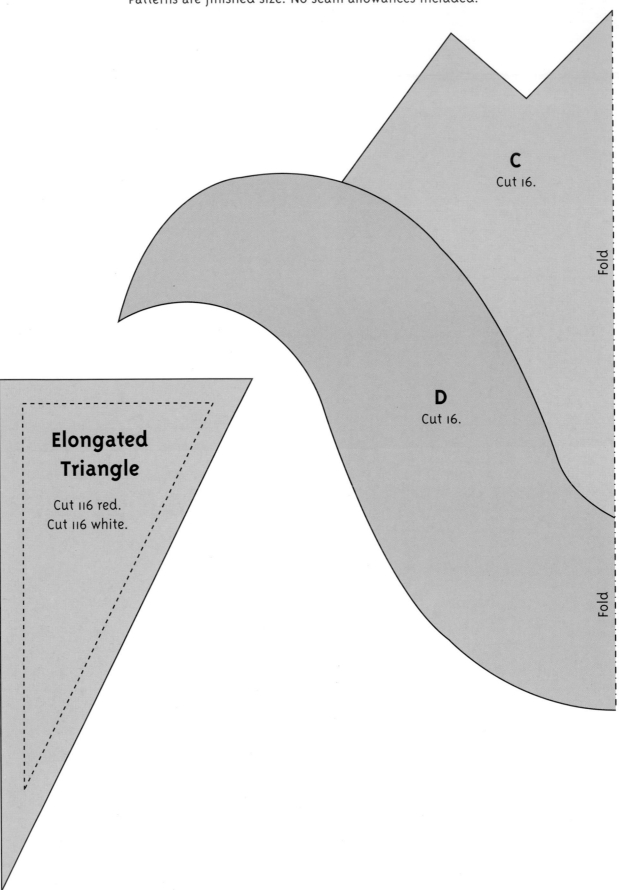

C
Cut 16.

Fold

D
Cut 16.

Fold

Elongated Triangle

Cut 116 red.
Cut 116 white.

Tulip Buds in Blue Vase

- Finished size: 60'' x 60''
- Finished block size: 25'' square
- Finished inside and outside sawtooth borders: 1¹/₄'' wide each
- Finished middle border: 2¹/₂'' wide

Pieced and appliquéd by Gwen Marston, Beaver Island, Michigan, 2003. Hand quilted by Frances Yoder.

I drew ideas for this quilt from an 1873 antique beauty that I discovered in the 1985 *Quilt Engagement Calendar*. I isolated, altered, and enlarged one small block from the lovely antique quilt and repeated it in a four-block format.

Two different red prints create a subtle illusion of depth in the pieced sawtooth border. The appliqués in the blocks are outline quilted, and the grounds are filled with a crosshatched grid. The pieced borders are outline quilted and the middle white border is quilted with a feather motif, which I drew freehand directly on the fabric.

Materials

Yardages are based on fabric that measures 40" wide after laundering.

- 4⅓ yards white fabric for block grounds, pieced border, middle border, and binding

- ½ yard red fabric for tulip appliqués

- Scraps of red fabric for berries

- ⅔ yard *total* of two different red fabrics for pieced border*

- 2 yards green fabric for stems and leaf appliqués

- ¼ yard blue fabric for flowerpot appliqués

- ½ yard yellow fabric for tulip, leaf, and flowerpot trim appliqués

- 3¾ yards fabric for backing

- 64" x 64" piece of batting

*You can use more of the tulip and berry fabric for one of these red fabrics.

Cutting

Cut strips across the fabric width (selvage to selvage).

From the white fabric:

- Cut 4 squares 25½" x 25½" for ground.

- Cut 6 strips 3" x width of fabric for middle border.

- Cut 7 strips 1¼" x width of fabric for binding.

- Cut 176 squares 2⅛" x 2⅛". Cut each square diagonally in one direction to make 352 half-square triangles for pieced borders.

From the green fabric:

- Cut 1¼"-wide strips from the bias of the fabric. You need 144" of bias for stems.

From the two different red fabrics:

- Cut a *total* of 176 squares 2⅛" x 2⅛". Cut each square diagonally in one direction to make 352 half-square triangles for pieced borders.

Appliquéing the Blocks

Block diagram

1. Refer to Making Bias Vines and Stems on page 44, and use the 1¼"-wide green fabric strips to make a single strip ⅝" x 144".

2. Use the method you prefer (either as described in Back to Basics: Cutting the Shapes on page 26 or using the patterns for pieces A–K on pages 75–78) to cut the following appliqué shapes:

   From red fabrics: 12 B and 12 E
   From green fabric: 4 each of C, D, F, G, H, and I
   From blue fabric: 4 K
   From yellow fabric: 12 A and 4 J

3. Refer to Back to Basics: Placing the Appliqué Patches (page 34), Back to Basics: Technique (page 39), the quilt photo on page 71, and the block diagram on page 72 to place and appliqué 12 stems to each 25½'' white square.

I butted the leaf appliqués up against the stems. Because a berry covers the area where the leaves and stems meet, I didn't need to turn under the ends of the leaves.

4. Refer to Needle-Turn Appliqué (page 40). Place and appliqué 3 each of A, B, and E and 1 each of C, D, F, G, H, I, J, and K to each block.

I used reverse appliqué (page 43) to add the yellow veins to the center of each F, G, H, and I leaf appliqué. Complete the reverse appliqué before sewing the leaves onto the quilt.

Quilt Assembly

1. Refer to the quilt photo on page 71. Arrange the blocks in 2 rows of 2 blocks each. Sew the blocks into rows. Press the seams in opposite directions from row to row. Sew the rows together. Press.

2. Sew white and red triangles together in pairs. Press. Make 352.

Make 352.

3. Sew 40 units from Step 2 to make a border, randomly mixing the two different red units. Press. Make 4.

Make 4.

4. Sew a border from Step 3 to the top and bottom of the quilt. Press the seams toward the borders.

5. Sew a unit from Step 2 to each end of a remaining pieced border strip. Press. Make 2.

Make 2.

6. Sew a border from Step 5 to the sides of the quilt top. Press the seams toward the borders.

7. Refer to Making Borders Fit Your Quilt (page 36) to sew the 3''-wide white middle border strips to the quilt, piecing them as necessary. Add top and bottom borders first, then side borders. Press the seams toward the white borders.

Two different red prints create a subtle illusion of depth in the pieced sawtooth border.

8. Sew 46 units from Step 2 to make a border, randomly mixing the two different red units. Press. Make 4.

Make 4.

9. Sew a border from Step 8 to the top and bottom of the quilt. Press the seams toward the borders.

10. Sew a unit from Step 2 to each end of a remaining pieced border strip. Press. Make 2.

Make 2.

11. Sew a border from Step 10 to the sides of the quilt top. Press the seams toward the borders.

Finishing

Refer to Helpful Information for Finishing Your Quilt (pages 86–89) to layer, baste, quilt, and finish the edges of your quilt. Use the 1¼" white fabric strips for binding.

Patterns are finished size. No seam allowances included.

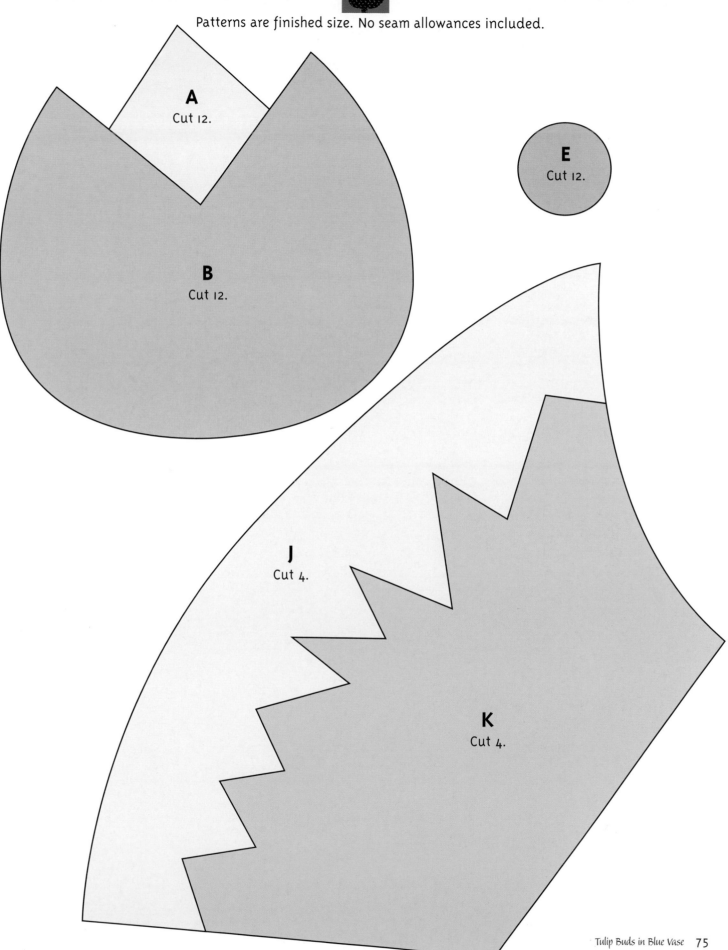

A
Cut 12.

B
Cut 12.

E
Cut 12.

J
Cut 4.

K
Cut 4.

Patterns are finished size. No seam allowances included.

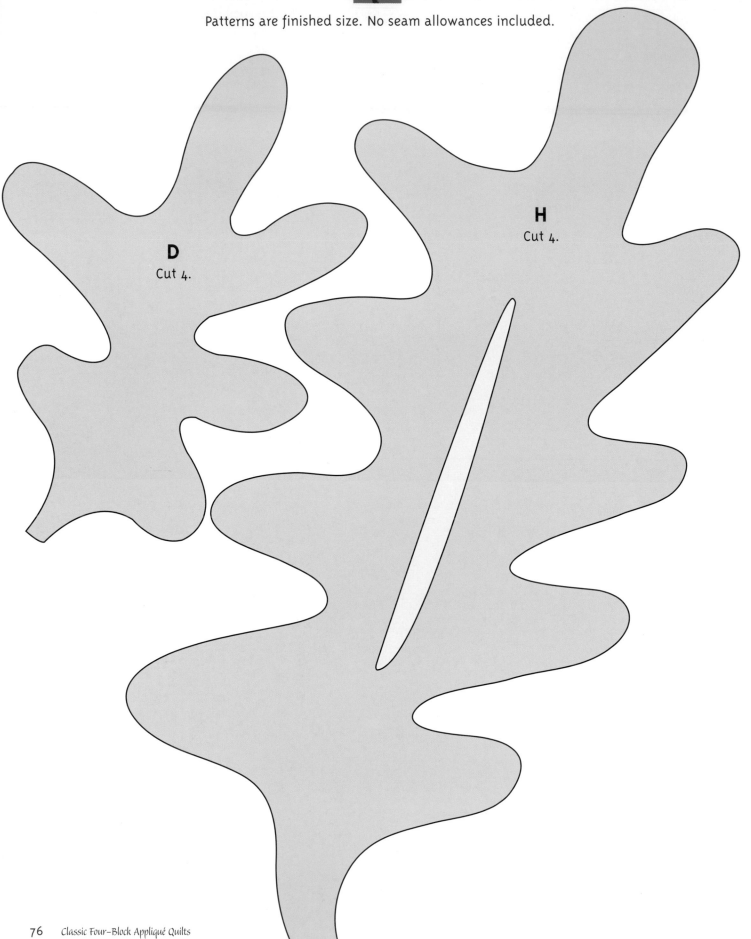

D
Cut 4.

H
Cut 4.

Patterns are finished size. No seam allowances included.

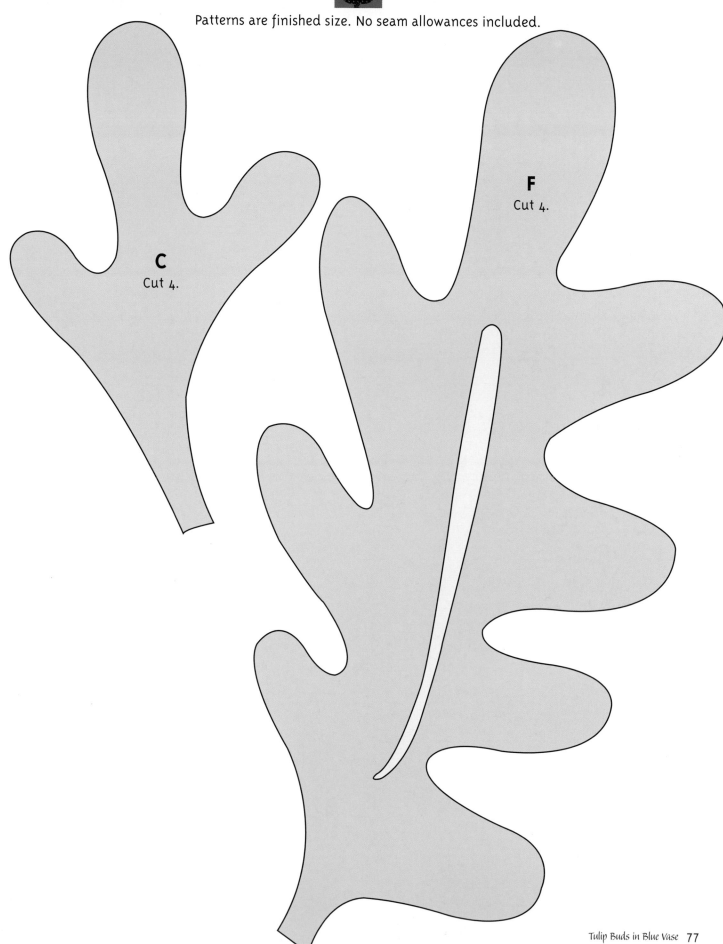

C
Cut 4.

F
Cut 4.

Patterns are finished size. No seam allowances included.

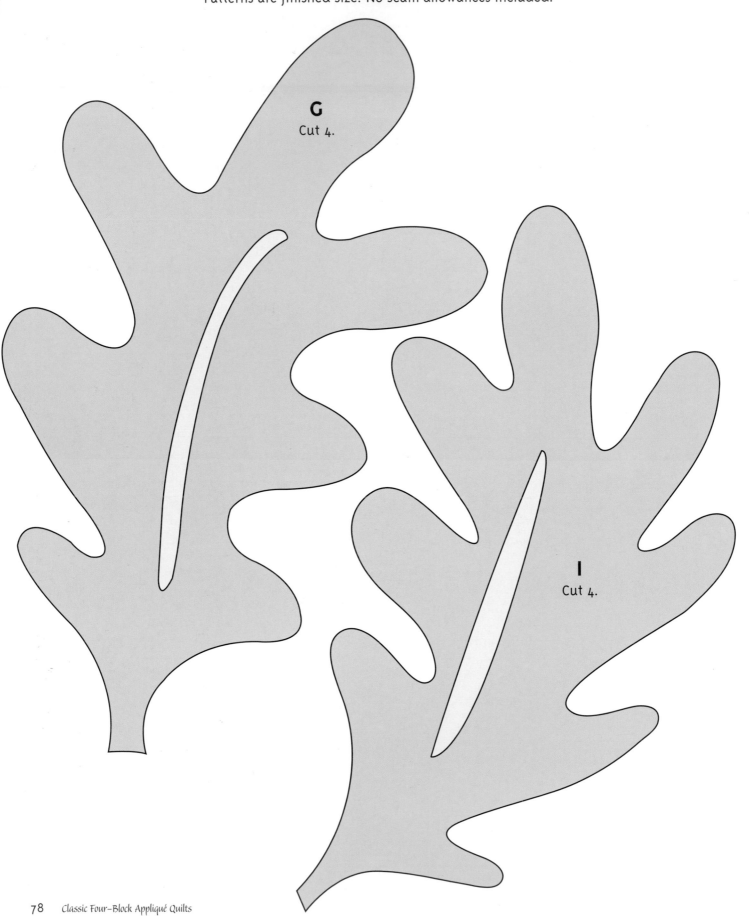

G

Cut 4.

I

Cut 4.

Adapting the Four-Block Quilt to a One-Block Format

The scale and bold design principles that make up the traditional four-block quilt are ideal for adapting to a one-block format. You can make a fantastic crib quilt by featuring one large, splashy block, with or without borders. I've used this idea repeatedly to make small quilts suitable for either crib or wall. Look at these one-block quilts to see the myriad ideas that you can use in your own work.

Horseshoe Plume includes both a narrow inner border and an appliqué border. I made the appliqué borders separately, with no attempt to turn the corners symmetrically, as was the method for many nineteenth-century appliqué quilts.

Although this is my original design, both the horseshoe plume shape and the center motif were part of a common nineteenth-century vocabulary. This quilt exhibits the allover quilting designs that are seen on earlier quilts but rarely used today. The crosshatched grid sneaks under the vine on the border but covers the rest of the quilt top, running right over the appliqués.

HORSESHOE PLUME, 48″ x 48″, pieced, appliquéd, and hand quilted by Gwen Marston, Beaver Island, Michigan, 1998.

Basket With Two Red Birds features a 34'' block corralled by a wide, energetic pieced border.

BASKET WITH TWO RED BIRDS, 44''x 44'', pieced, appliquéd, and hand quilted by Gwen Marston, Beaver Island, Michigan, 1998.

Three different prints and a solid, all left over from other projects, make up the stems on this quilt. The floral shapes are the same as those in **Tulip With Red-Tipped Leaves** (page 93). The quilted grid runs over most of the appliqué, recreating one of my favorite treatments from antique quilts.

Multiple borders, both pieced and appliquéd, became the solution for *Flower Pot* and *Basket With Berry Border* (page 82). Notice that all four appliqué borders on *Flower Pot* are different. Although there is no exact repeat, the shapes and colors are similar, so the result is both harmonious and unexpected.

FLOWER POT, 40″ × 40″, pieced, appliquéd, and hand quilted by Gwen Marston, Beaver Island, Michigan, 1995.

This quilt features two old-fashioned quilting ideas. One is the double hanging-diamond grid quilted behind the central block. The other involves the feathers that come off the border vine. The diamond-shaped leaves and the four different appliqué borders are also ideas that I borrowed from nineteenth-century quilts.

The idea for *Basket With Berry Border* came from one block in a sampler quilt made around 1850 and shown in *Ladies Circle Patchwork Quilts*. It is a classic example of enlarging a smaller block to a grand scale to create either a one-block or possibly a four-block quilt. In fact, any appliqué block you see is a possible candidate for enlargement.

This quilt is one of my favorites. The rather bizarre block design captured my interest immediately because of its primitive and surprising shapes. It has always reminded me of Marge Simpson holding her arms up in the air and shouting, "Help me! Help me!" The original block was later featured on the cover of *West Virginia Quilts and Quiltmakers*, by Fawn Valentine (see Bibliography on page 110).

The sawtooth border in this quilt includes various tones of red, creating a sense of depth. To capture the flavor of a mid-nineteenth-century quilt, I quilted double-lined abstract floral shapes and leaves in the body of the quilt. I then quilted close diagonals behind these designs. The outer border is quilted with triple-lined diagonals.

BASKET WITH BERRY BORDER, 50'' x 50'', pieced, appliquéd, and hand quilted by Gwen Marston, Beaver Island, Michigan, 1999.

Whig Rose has lots to look at. The idea for the rather primitive block came from a circa-1860 Pennsylvania quilt that appeared in the 1996 *Quilt Engagement Calendar*. I borrowed the idea for completely different border designs from my favorite quilter, Susan McCord (see page 14). About a dozen of her stunning quilts are housed at The Henry Ford Museum in Dearborn, Michigan, including two nine-block appliqués, each with four different appliqué borders.

Diversifying the borders is an excellent way to add interest to any quilt. In this case, I quilted my name and the date between the birds on the bottom border, which I dare say is a good way to kill two birds with one stone, as the quilting accomplishes both signing and dating.

WHIG ROSE, 40" x 40½", pieced, appliquéd, and hand quilted by Gwen Marston, Beaver Island, Michigan, 1996.

This simplified version of a much-loved pattern is made more interesting with three different appliqué borders and a variety of organic quilting designs to fill in the open areas. I did not mark the grid; consequently, it is somewhat inconsistent. I've seen this practical characteristic fairly frequently in antique quilts. The irregular lines give a very faint, but effective, sense of movement. In my view, they also give the quilt a distinguishing appearance. The quilting motif in the gold borders was scratched with my needle as I worked.

Occasionally, I connect instantly with a picture of an antique quilt. In most cases, I eventually get around to making a quilt along similar lines. The inspiration for this quilt was a crib quilt from Pennsylvania made around 1865 and shown in the 1992 *Quilt Engagement Calendar*. The shape of the tulip should tell you why I nicknamed this quilt "The Foot Tulip."

Tulip With Dogtooth Border has exactly that—a dogtooth border—replicating the original antique quilt. I made the dogtooth edge by cutting fabric the length of the sides of the quilt, folding it in half repeatedly, and cutting a point. Naturally, I couldn't fold the entire length into a 1½" unit, so I folded it as much as I could and still cut the fabric. This folded-fabric method allowed me to capture the irregularities and slightly curved edges characteristic of the dogtooth borders seen on antique quilts.

Sue Nickels gets the credit for choosing the wonderful quilting designs and for masterfully machine quilting beautiful feathers around all the leaves and inside the center motif and tulips in this quilt.

TULIP WITH DOGTOOTH BORDER, 36" x 36", pieced and appliquéd by Gwen Marston, Beaver Island, Michigan, 1999. Machine quilted by Sue Nickels.

Here's a final idea for you to ponder! You can make a good-sized one-block quilt by adding wide borders to a single large block. *Gwenny's Crossed Tulips* started out as one large block with an uncertain future. I've long been interested in oversized appliqué blocks, and this one was made on an impulse. It remained single until I decided to use it as the center for a personal quilt about things that have brought me great joy. I made shapes representing motherhood, my children, and the dogs and horses in my life. Notice the dogtooth border on the edge of this quilt, with all of its classic irregularities—the result of using the nineteenth-century technique of cutting directly from folded fabric.

The entire process of making this quilt was a joyful one. It is all about the things that have enriched my life and brought me happiness. As a result, I counted my blessings the entire time I worked on this quilt. To this day, I am very happy to have this special quilt to enjoy.

GWENNY'S CROSSED TULIPS, 64'' x 64'', pieced, appliquéd, and hand quilted by Gwen Marston, Beaver Island, Michigan, 1992.

So—in summary—it's all up to you. Any of the four-block quilts shown in this book could easily be altered to make a one-block quilt. Similarly, all of these one-block quilts could easily grow into four blocks. All you need to do is stitch three more blocks.

Helpful Information for Finishing Your Quilt

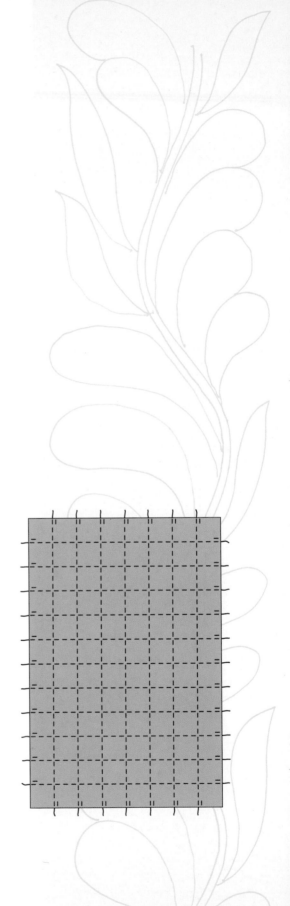

Backing

Cut your backing approximately 4" larger than your finished quilt top. If you need to piece the backing to make it large enough, remember that there are no rules about how the backing should be pieced. Quilters have traditionally chosen the most practical and obvious way to piece the backings for their quilts.

Batting

I prefer to use 100% cotton batting in my quilts because—surprise!—I like the look of antique quilts, and I like natural fibers. Others prefer polyester batting because of its loft and because it is easier to needle and doesn't need to be quilted as closely as cotton.

I cut the batting by layering it over the stretched backing, smoothing it out, and trimming the excess. This method requires no measuring.

Layering and Basting

Having learned to quilt from Mennonite women, I quilt in a full-size frame that does not require basting. Most of today's quilters, however, quilt in a hoop or portable frame that does require basting. Here is one method to use for layering and basting your quilt.

Press the backing and the quilt top, clipping any stray threads. Spread the backing right side down on a clean, flat surface. Secure the edges with masking tape or T-pins. Center and smooth the batting, and then the quilt top, right side up over the backing.

If you plan to hand quilt, baste the layers together with a long needle and light-colored thread. Baste the vertical and horizontal centerlines first, then baste in a grid with lines of stitches no more than 3"–4" apart. Finish by basting around the entire perimeter of the quilt top.

If you plan to machine quilt, repeat the process, substituting small, rustproof safety pins for the needle and thread.

I used a typical nineteenth-century combination of outline quilting and background filler of diagonal lines for the blocks in **Rose and Pomegranate**. For a full view of this quilt, see page 55.

Quilting

As with every other design phase, I look to antique four-block appliqué quilts for guidance in choosing the quilting designs for my four-block quilts. I often outline the appliqué shapes and fill in the backgrounds with crosshatched grids or other linear fill designs.

I also enjoy adapting feather, leaf, plume, and floral motifs from old quilts, often drawing them freehand, particularly in borders. You'll find some of my favorites scattered throughout this book. Use these as inspiration—or draw your own!

Binding

The majority of nineteenth-century quilts were bound with a single-fold binding cut on the straight of the goods. This is my preference, as well. A single-fold binding is easy to handle and gives a fine finished line to the edge of the quilt. The double-fold binding so popular today seems too bulky for my taste.

1. Carefully trim the batting and backing even with the edge of the quilt top on all sides.

2. Use a rotary cutter and a sturdy ruler to cut the necessary number of strips 1¼" wide. Join the strips with a diagonal seam; this helps the finished seam lie flat.

3. Align the binding with the raw edge of the quilt top, right sides together. Leaving the first few inches of binding unsewn, stitch the binding to the quilt with a ¼"-wide seam.

4. To miter the corners, sew to exactly ¼" from the corner of the quilt. Backstitch, lift the presser foot, and pull the quilt away from the sewing machine. Fold the binding up and away from the quilt at a 45° angle as shown.

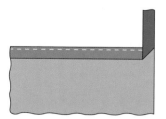

5. Fold the binding down, and carefully resume stitching with a ¼''-wide seam exactly ¼'' from the corner. Continue in this manner until you have turned the final corner.

Start stitching ¼'' from corner.

6. Stop sewing about 5'' from the place where you began attaching the binding to the quilt. Remove the quilt from the sewing machine. Place both ends of the binding along the edge of the quilt, and overlap the ends. Draw a pencil line at a 45° angle along the edge of the binding strip on top. Trim the strip ½'' past the drawn line.

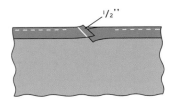

½''

7. Join the ends of the binding with a ½''-wide seam. Finger press the seam open. Finish stitching the binding to the quilt.

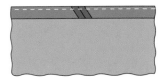

8. Bring the binding to the back of the quilt, fold the raw edge of the binding under, and hand stitch the binding in place with thread that matches the quilt's outermost border. This keeps the stitches invisible in case you inadvertently stitch through to the quilt top.

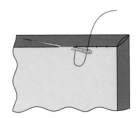

Finishing Without Binding

In the past, bringing the quilt backing around to the front of the quilt was a popular way to finish the edges. The raw edge of the backing was folded under and either hand stitched or topstitched in place by machine. This method of finishing made sense because it saved fabric: no additional fabric was needed for a separate binding. Although not common today, this method seems especially appropriate for quilts made in the back-to-basics style.

Follow these steps with care. Don't rush! Take your time to trim the batting and backing accurately.

1. Use scissors to carefully trim the batting even with the edge of the quilt top on all sides.

2. Use a rotary cutter and a sturdy ruler to trim the backing ¾" from the edge of the quilt top and batting on all sides.

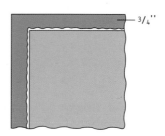

3. Fold the backing to the front of the quilt so the raw edge of the backing meets the raw edge of the quilt top. Fold the edge over again to create a finished edge as shown. Pin generously (approximately every 2½").

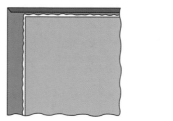

4. Use matching thread to sew the edge down by hand or machine as shown.

Gallery of Quilts

The quilts in this gallery
include those I have made,
quilts made by friends
and students, and antique
quilts from my personal
collection and the collections
of generous friends and
museums.

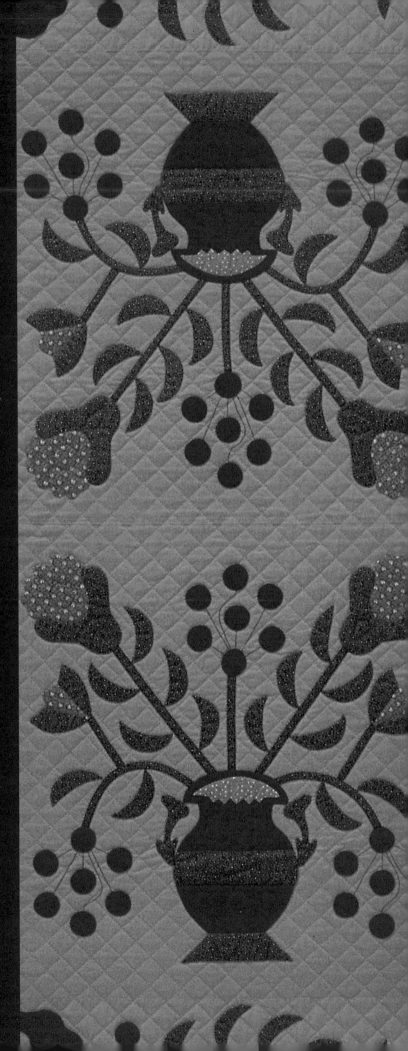

EAGLE, 79″ x 79″, pieced, appliquéd, and hand quilted by Gwen Marston, Beaver Island, Michigan, 1986.

Taking my cues from classic eagle quilts, I began designing this quilt by drawing the eagle on butcher paper and cutting up the paper drawing to make my templates. Instead of using one wing pattern, I used two, allowing the right and left wings to be slightly different. I cut the stars and center sunbursts from folded fabric, which accounts for the obvious irregularities. After cutting out the large sunburst, I used the circle I'd cut from its center as my guide for making the inner sunburst fit properly.

I quilted the blocks by crosshatching right across the appliqué. The sawtooth border is outline quilted, and I drew a continuous feather freehand to grace the border.

TULIP WITH RED-TIPPED LEAVES, 72" x 72", pieced and appliquéd by Gwen Marston, Beaver Island, Michigan, 2002. Hand quilted by Carol Morris.

Working from a rough sketch, I cut the shapes and laid out the block as a design demonstration in an appliqué class. A similar demonstration resulted in a sister quilt, **Basket With Two Red Birds** (page 80).

I traveled with this quilt, using it to demonstrate appliqué technique in my classes. It took about three years, but I eventually completed all of the appliqué while on the road. I would take just one block and my little sketch to remind me roughly of where everything went; however, with the other blocks at home, I had to sew the shapes on where I thought they should go. If you look carefully, you will find a lot of variation in the positioning of the shapes.

The very beautiful quilting designs came from a circa-1820 quilt owned by my mentor, Mary Schafer.

This quilt holds lots of surprises, as did many of the appliqué quilts from earlier times. I began sewing three berries on each side of each lower stem, but then I changed my mind and did the rest four to a side. Two blue leaves hide among the many green ones. Some of the birds have top notches, turning them into California quail, and the diagonal lines and double-feathered wreaths are quilted right over the appliqué.

TULIP POT AND CHERRIES, 66'' x 66'', pieced, appliquéd, and hand quilted by Gwen Marston, Beaver Island, Michigan, 1987. Collection of Brenda Marston.

Here is a good example of how free placement of shapes can create a playful, folk-art sensibility for a quilt. I sewed the stems with no attempt to make them resemble each other, and I added the berries until I felt there were enough. The body of the quilt is quilted with free-form leaf shapes, and feathers "grow" from the vine on the border.

TULIPS AND BERRIES IN VASE, 60'' x 64'', pieced, appliquéd, and hand quilted by Gwen Marston, Beaver Island, Michigan, 1992.

I made this quilt one day when I decided to take a day off and do anything I wanted. When I asked myself what I would most like to do, I answered, "Make a four-block quilt!" Just for the fun of it, I played with atypical colors, unlike any you might expect to see in a nineteenth-century design. Using my back-to-basics methods, I had the quilt designed and cut out, the stems sewn on, and had already started working on the baskets by the end of the day.

I cut the swag border from folded fabric. I pressed the seam allowance under, pinned it to the border, and topstitched it with matching thread. The quilt is quilted in an allover fan pattern.

APRICOT FLOWER POT, 58'' x 58'', pieced, appliquéd, and hand quilted by Gwen Marston, Beaver Island, Michigan, 1996.

Mary was inspired to make this quilt by an antique block that she spotted (and was graciously permitted to photograph) at the annual Houston Quilt Festival. The background on the original was muslin, but Mary decided to use cheddar instead. She began the quilt at one of my Beaver Island Quilt Retreats. She designed her own border, using dates and initials, much as I (and our foremothers) have been inspired to do.

FOUR-BLOCK APPLIQUÉ FLOWER POT, 72'' x 72'', pieced and appliquéd by Mary Hovey, Rosebush, Michigan. Hand quilted by Elsie Vredenberg, Tustin, Michigan, 1999.

TULIP FOUR BLOCK, 76" x 76", pieced and appliquéd by Cathy Jones, Grand Rapids, Michigan. Machine quilted by Prairie Star Quilts, Iowa, 2002.

Cathy was inspired to create this original design at a Beaver Island Quilt Retreat after viewing many of my antique four-block quilts. The entire quilt is hand appliquéd, with the exception of the stems which were machine stitched. Cathy mistakenly cut into the white background when stitching the very first block, but was open to my advice to "just appliqué over the cut." If you look in the lower right corner, you will see two red birds. Guess which one hides the "mistake?"

This quilt top is an original design based on several nineteenth-century Whig Rose quilts. Lois began it as she was planning a vacation and realized she had no appliqué project to carry along. Within a week, she had the block designed, the motifs cut, and one block prepared to appliqué. The top was completed over the next year, mostly on airplane and auto trips. She admits the many hand-stitched cherries—which she claims are in my honor—and the dogtooth border were a challenge, but she is justifiably pleased with the results. She plans lots of fancy, hand-quilted feathers, with closely cross-hatched background filler.

WHIG ROSE (quilt top), 80'' x 80'', pieced and appliquéd by Lois Griffith, Cove Creek, Arizona, 2004.

This quilt is based on a nineteenth-century folk-art block made by an anonymous quilter. The simplicity of the block and its unusual colors appealed to Lois from the first time she saw it. She designed four borders to echo the block motifs, but ran out of the white background fabric when she came to the top border. Inspired by nineteenth-century quilts she had seen, Lois decided that was not a problem, and eliminated the top border altogether. She pays further homage to the nineteenth century by tucking a narrow cheddar piping between the binding and the quilt.

FLOWER POT, 85'' x 85½'', pieced, appliquéd, and hand quilted by Lois Griffith, Cove Creek, Arizona, 2004.

Jeannette's four-block quilt was inspired by a very old baby quilt she saw at a friend's home in Chicago. The original was one-fourth the size of Jeannette's version, and the leaves were not appliquéd but quilted. It was her idea to use four blocks as the central medallion, to appliqué the leaves, and to add the sawtooth border—all good choices, don't you think?

CROSSED TULIPS, 65'' x 65'', pieced, appliquéd, and hand quilted by Jeannette McKim, Columbus, Indiana, 2003.

It's easy to see that nary a rose is like any other rose. In this quilt, overall fan quilting rules the day. However, there are also individual feathers alternating in single- and double-lined quilting in the red sections of the large red center roses and in a line of feathers in the narrow sashing between the blocks. The unknown quilter also managed to arrange the fans to create a concentric circle in the center of the quilt.

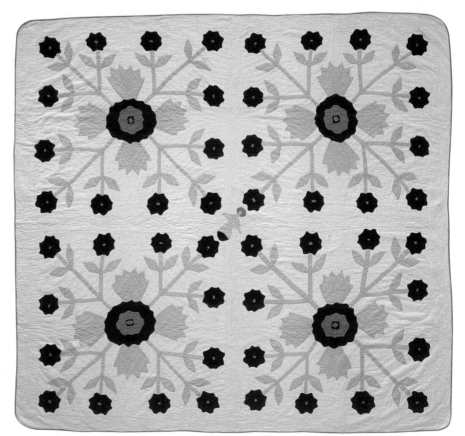

ROSE, 74'' x 78'', circa 1890, Indiana, quiltmaker unknown. Collection of Gwen Marston. Shown in exhibit of Marston Antique Quilts, Tokyo, Japan, in 1997.

BEAVER ISLAND FOUR BLOCK, 93″ x 103″, pieced, appliquéd, and hand quilted by Karen Selta, Lansing, Michigan, 2002.

Karen drew her inspiration from a Whig Rose quilt she saw in a circa 1975 quilt book. She wasn't crazy about the flowers, so she substituted Coxcombs instead. She used black for the background because she admires Amish quilts and "because black doesn't show the dirt."

Karen began this quilt at one of my Beaver Island Quilt Retreats. It took a bit more time to complete than she expected, but I have no doubt that Karen—and you—will agree that it was well worth the time and effort.

The original fabrics in half of the plumes, as well as in other areas of this quilt, have faded over time. Notice how each plume has a distinct personality due to the free placement of shapes. This feature alone sets this quilt in motion, with the abstract floral shapes providing an extra spark. The appliqué and quilting stitches are clear evidence that this is the work of an expert quilter. I like everything about this quilt!

PLUME, 77'' x 77'', circa 1865–1875, Iowa, quiltmaker unknown. Collection of Gwen Marston. Shown in exhibit of Marston Antique Quilts, Tokyo, Japan, in 1997.

Here are all of the characteristics of quilts from this period rolled into one wonderful quilt: free placement of shapes, unresolved corners, lots of quilting, and a typical color scheme. The edges were finished by bringing the quilt top around to the back of the quilt, taking bits of the border roses with it.

PRINCESS FEATHER, 80'' x 82'', circa 1850, Illinois, quiltmaker unknown. Collection of Gwen Marston. Shown in exhibit of Marston Antique Quilts, Tokyo, Japan, in 1997.

WHIG ROSE, 84''x 84'', circa 1900, found in Michigan, quiltmaker unknown. Collection of Gwen Marston. Shown in exhibit of Marston Antique Quilts, Tokyo, Japan, in 1997.

This hand-appliquéd and hand-pieced quilt is machine quilted in a square grid that runs over the quilt's entire surface.

While four-block quilts enjoyed their heyday in the mid-nineteenth century, they continued to be made well past that time, as this "rough" summer spread reminds us.

WHIG ROSE SUMMER SPREAD, 65" x 73", circa 1940, found in Indiana, quiltmaker unknown. Collection of Gwen Marston.

Biz bought this quirky quilt top on eBay, and has since entertained many interesting speculations from family, friends, and quilting experts concerning its rather eccentric design! It appears to date from the mid-1800s and has never been laundered. The fabric is still supple, however, so she hopes to quilt it someday.

UNTITLED FOUR BLOCK (quilt top), 65" x 73", provenance unknown. Collection of Biz Storm.

Plume appears to be an older quilt that was quilted at a later date. The hand-applied red binding is a different fabric than any other in the quilt, which also suggests a later finish. The quilting thread is white, and the stitches measure about seven to the inch. Some of the green fabric has faded in spots, but otherwise it shows no signs of wear at all, so it was likely never used. Deb displays this quilt in her living room each holiday season for her friends and family to enjoy.

PLUME, 82'' x 82'', provenance unknown. Collection of Deb Ballard.

WHIG ROSE, 89'' x 90'', circa 1850, Pennsylvania, quiltmaker unknown. From the Mary Shafer Collection, Michigan State University Museum, East Lansing, Michigan. Photo courtesy of Michigan State University Museum.

Mary Shafer bought this quilt, along with a similar one with white background, at the same time from the same dealer. The two quilts were very much alike in pattern, style, and the use of small-scale prints for the background. However, while the white quilt featured wreath, pineapple, pinwheel, rosette, and other more detailed quilting motifs, the quilt pictured here is quilted rather simply. It is crosshatched and includes a cable motif that runs off the ends of the quilt, typical of the period.

Betty Harriman (1890–1971) was a serious quilt historian and prolific quiltmaker from Bunceton, Missouri. When she died, Michigan quiltmaker Mary Shafer acquired Betty's unfinished work and completed many of Betty's "starts," including this beautiful quilt.

A note from Betty found attached to the quilt top credits this pattern to the Krockman family.

YORK COUNTY, 92" x 92", circa 1963, pieced and appliquéd by Betty H. Harriman, Bunceton, Missouri. Marked by Betty Harriman and Mary Shafer. Completed by Mary Shafer, 1999. From the Mary Shafer Collection, Michigan State University Museum, East Lansing, Michigan. Photo courtesy of Michigan State University Museum.

This is another of the Harriman/Shafer collaborations. In this case, Betty made the block, and Mary designed the center and border appliqué motifs and had the quilt finished. Both women were interested in making historically correct quilts; that is, traditional quilts made in the style of a particular time.

WASHINGTON PLUME, 90" x 96", blocks appliquéd by Betty Harriman, Bunceton, Missouri, 1965. Additional appliqué by Mary Shafer. From the Mary Shafer Collection, Michigan State University Museum, East Lansing, Michigan. Photo courtesy of Michigan State University Museum.

WREATH AND BERRIES, 66'' x 66'', pieced, appliquéd, and hand quilted by Gwen Marston, Beaver Island, Michigan, 1996.

The background for this quilt is white linen. I have used berries in many of my quilts because I believe you get a lot for your money with them. For this quilt, I wondered, "If some berries are good, wouldn't a lot be even better?" I have to admit that part way through appliquéing all of these berries, I began to question the wisdom of my logic! Now that the quilt is finished, however, I'm very pleased with the results. The quilting is as basic as it gets: the appliqué shapes are outline quilted, and the background is filled with cross-hatching.

COXCOMB, 73" x 80", pieced and appliquéd by Gwen Marston, Beaver Island, Michigan. Hand quilted by Gwen Marston and Joe Cunningham, 1984.

I cut the pattern for this quilt from folded paper. I folded the paper into eighths, sketched one-eighth of the design (freehand, of course!), and cut out the shape. A touch of reverse appliqué in the "combs" adds a nice spark to this simple design.

This is a paper-cut pattern similar to many quilts made in the mid-nineteenth century. I cut the center reel shape from paper that I folded into eighths. I machine stitched the tulips and leaves to the center reel and then appliquéd the entire motif in place.

TULIP AND OAK LEAF, 75'' x 75'', pieced and appliquéd by Gwen Marston, Beaver Island, Michigan. Hand quilted by Gwen Marston and Joe Cunningham, 1987.

Like **Coxcomb** (page 106), this design was cut from folded paper.

BLUE TULIP, 76'' x 76'', pieced and appliquéd by Gwen Marston, Beaver Island, Michigan. Hand quilted by Gwen Marston and Joe Cunningham, 1990. Collection of Mary Whaley.

Afterword

When all is said and done, we must each find our own way. It is my hope that this book will suggest some alternative routes for you to explore in your quiltmaking. If you haven't been down this road before, start with a day trip; that is, a small, manageable project. You don't have to wander off into totally uncharted territory. Let antique quilts serve as your road map. There are many old quilts to show places you may want to visit. The main thing, of course, is that you enjoy the trip!

Bibliography

Bacon, Lenice. *American Patchwork Quilts*. New York: William Morrow & Company, 1973.

Bassett, Lynne Z., and Jack Larkin. *Northern Comfort: New England's Early Quilts, 1780–1850*. Nashville, TN: Rutledge Hill Press, 1998.

Bishop, Robert, and Carleton L. Safford. *America's Quilts and Coverlets*. New York: Weathervane Books, 1974.

———. *New Discoveries in American Quilts*. New York: E.P. Dutton, 1975.

Bresenhan, Karoline Patterson, and Nancy O'Bryant Puentes. *Lone Stars: A Legacy of Texas Quilts, 1836–1936*. Austin: University of Texas Press, 1986.

Clark, Ricky. *Quilted Gardens: Floral Quilts of the Nineteenth Century*. Nashville, TN: Rutledge Hill Press, 1994.

Clark, Ricky, George W. Knepper, and Ellice Ronsheim. *Quilts in Community: Ohio's Traditions*. Nashville, TN: Rutledge Hill Press, 1991.

Finley, Ruth E. *Old Patchwork Quilts*. Philadelphia: J.B. Lippincott, 1929.

Fox, Sandi. *19th Century American Quilt*. Japan: The Seibu Museum of Art, 1984.

———. *Quilts: California Bound, California Made 1840–1940*. Los Angeles: FIDM, 2002.

———. *Small Endearments: 19th-Century Quilts for Children*. New York: Charles Scribner's Sons, 1985.

Hall, Carrie A., and Rose Kretzinger. *The Romance of the Patchwork Quilt in America*. Caldwell, ID: Caxton Printers, Bonanza Books, 1935.

Helen Foresman Spencer Museum of Art. *Quilter's Choice*. Lawrence, KS, 1978.

Johnson, Mary Elizabeth. *Mississippi Quilts*. Jackson: University Press of Mississippi, 2001.

Kiracofe, Roderick. *The American Quilt*. New York: Clarkson Potter, 1993.

Lasansky, Jeannette. *Pieced by Mother: Over 100 Years of Quiltmaking Traditions*. Lewisberg, PA: Union County Historical Society, 1987.

Marston, Gwen. *Mary Schafer: American Quiltmaker*. Ann Arbor: University of Michigan Press, 2004.

Ramsey, Bets, and Merikay Waldvogel. *The Quilts of Tennessee*. Nashville, TN: Rutledge Hill Press, 1986.

Valentine, Fawn. *West Virginia Quilts and Quiltmakers*. Athens: Ohio University Press, 2000.

Woodard, Thomas K., and Blanche Greenstein. *Crib Quilts and Other Small Wonders*. New York: E.P. Dutton, 1981.

About the Author

Gwen Marston is a quiltmaker who has had many exhibits in the United States and one in Japan. She learned to make quilts from a group of Mennonite women and still uses traditional methods to create her work. She lectures and teaches quiltmaking around the country and has hosted quilt retreats in northern Michigan for the past 22 years. This is her eighteenth book.

Another C&T book by
Gwen Marston:

For more information, ask for a free catalog:
C&T Publishing, Inc.
P.O. Box 1456
Lafayette, CA 94549
(800) 284-1114
Email: ctinfo@ctpub.com
Website: www.ctpub.com

For quilting supplies:
Cotton Patch Mail Order
3405 Hall Lane, Dept.CTB
Lafayette, CA 94549
(800) 835-4418
(925) 283-7883
Email: quiltusa@yahoo.com
Website: www.quiltusa.com

Index